It's All Pretty Silly Really Anyway Isn't It?

A Memoir of Sorts ... And Then Some

Bill Grivna

ISBN-10: 154538505X

ISBN-13: 978-1545385050

Cover Design by: Rosemary Christian

DEDICATION

To all the amazing people in my life, including the very dearest of friends, who do not appear in the selections of this book but who have also enhanced my journey so immeasurably.

Contents

Acknowledgements

I have been blessed with having a number of friends who are also fine writers. I want to thank all of them for their thoughts and encouragements, particularly Ed Jacobitti who first floated the idea that I try writing by penning a short story about my father. That first "tale" was the genesis of this little book.

Other writer/friends to thank are Steve Brown, Jeff Skoblow, Scott Sheperd, Kathleen Donovan, and Brenda Mezz. I also want to give my deepest heart-felt thanks to my lovely and talented wife, Rosemary, whose ready ear and excellent ideas, as well as formatting and editing skills, have made this book possible.

Finally, to all those special people referred to in this book—though nameless, you will probably know who you are—I want to thank you for so enriching my life. My love and gratitude to you all.

Introduction

How did this odd little book come about? Hard to say.
It seems to have emerged rather spontaneously in these
little snippets of tales (Part I) and musings (Part II) from a
mind that had seldom expressed itself in writing anything
personal, until now. I'm probably the only full professor
who managed to escape thirty years of academia without
writing a single journal article, let alone an entire book.

With age comes reflection, I guess, and a mini-urge to
leave some kind of proverbial record behind. Besides,
once these little bursts of memory started to slip into my
consciousness, often as I first dreamily awakened, this
kind of writing began to be fun. What could be better than
that?

As it turns out, this book is not about specific,
traditional career achievements in my life, of which, I'm
happy to say, there were at least a few, but rather it's
about the most personally affecting and memorable
events on my journey. And, as my wife has suggested, it's
a testament to how amazing it is that it all turned out so
well. To my readers, whoever you may be, thanks for the
opportunity to share my adventures with you.

PART ONE:

Tales of Billy Joe

(Glimpses through the Haze)

I. SOME EARLY STUFF

Cable Cars and Christmas Carols

It started out as a Merry Christmas caroling party on a rented imitation cable car on a chilly December night in San Francisco. A bit of an odd event in itself. But it became a "how-many-things-can-go-wrong-in-one-night-in-some-really-terrible-ways-but-which-seem-pretty-funny-now" kind of event.

So, here are some images from that goofy, fuzzy night: Young, late 20s, artistic, fun-loving people partying in a large, charming San Francisco hill-top apartment, with cozy fireplace, and libations and pot in abundance. Merriment.

Then, a rented cable car (on wheels) materializes ... all aboard! Christmas music blares over the speaker system, partiers sing along, and the cable car moves out to tour and bring holiday joy to the neighborhoods. Good Will to Man!

But. There was one last stop to make, to pick up two more couples on the way.

Then, me, already a bit stoned and tipsy, lunging forth to greet one of the new arrivals, a buddy, with a spirited holiday bear hug. This maneuver results in both my friend and I falling backward and crashing into a solid glass window. The back of my head is about to be in serious trouble. Instead, my noble friend puts his arm around the back of my head to protect me, and as we smash into the window, shattering it—it is his hand and arm that are seriously bloodied, and still bleeding heavily. Stunned silence on board.

Soon, "Where's the nearest hospital?" someone shouts. Off we go. I'm dazed. My friend is brought into the emergency room, via an open-air courtyard, lit by a single, large overhead street lamp. It's snowing now, lightly, creating an eerie, yet strangely beautiful glow with the street light. Silence.

Filled with total guilt and remorse, I lurch out of the cable car, running to the center of the courtyard, then screaming my friend's name, not unlike Brando in "Streetcar." Friends grab me. I'm pulled back onto the cable car. We wait.

It's determined that our injured friend will be OK after some more treatment, and he and his wife will take a cab home later. The caroling will be abandoned, and the rest of us will return to the party apartment on the hill, and try to regain some sense of holiday gaiety.

That, apparently, does not work for me. I am found, I am told later, outside the apartment, trying to karate chop the branches off an evergreen tree growing there. The irony of it being a "Christmas tree" escapes me at the time, I think. I am brought upstairs to rejoin the festivities. Not feeling particularly cheery, I find myself hiding in a corner of the bedroom, in the dark. I need to escape. I sneak into the kitchen and grab one premixed bottle each of an eggnog drink, and a spiced brandy cocktail. To alleviate my shame and guilt, I sneak back into the bedroom, and retrieve a spiritual LP record, that I had given the hostess, my girlfriend, at an earlier point in time. Then I slither, unseen, out the door ... down the hill to my little room (a walk-in closet actually, but that's another tale) in a communal flat where I reside.

I place the record, standing upright, on top of my only furniture piece, a bureau, with the two liquor bottles framing the LP, like candlesticks surrounding a painting over a fireplace. Also, a kind of shrine. To what?

I lie down on my small, single mattress, still in my clothes, arms folded across my chest. I close my eyes, trying to fade out ... seeking some kind of peace. Merry Christmas.

Way Back When ... Reading Stories

I'm very, very young. I'm snuggled onto Mommy's lap or hugging to her side with her arm around me. I'm warm and safe, and she's reading me a story. I love stories. I love when she reads to me. It makes me happy.

This story is magical. Lots of tigers chasing each other in a circle, and then turning into butter, and putting the tiger-butter onto pancakes! How can this be? Only years later did I learn about racism, and the controversies over *Little Black Sambo*.

There was no racism in NordEast Minneapolis when I was growing up ... or so I thought, because there were absolutely no black people there. "They" were all living across the river on the North Side, or just past downtown on the South Side, and we played against them in basketball and football, but not much in tennis.

And, my mother always said that everybody was equal, and we should always treat people who seemed different, just like everyone else. Curled up in my mother's arms there was no racism, there was only a book and big, colorful pictures of a little boy, and tigers that ran fast and turned into butter.

The Mystery Man at the Train Station

Very sleepy-late. A dark, chilly and windy night.
We're all bundled up.

Going with Mommy to meet someone new called Daddy.
In a Taxi car! It's a place called Train Station.
I'm excited, but it's scary too.
He's a Soldier.

Many years later, my two and a half year old self from that train station evening, is a full-fledged adult, who has had many more encounters with the Mystery Man Soldier. My mom divorced my dad when I was thirteen. Alcoholism.

Joe Bright and NordEast

We never had a car. Good thing probably. My dad, nicknamed Joe Bright, drank a lot. But he was good guy, well-liked by his many buddies, who thought he was smart.

Walking with Dad around our home streets of NordEast Minneapolis as it was affectionately called by all in our neighborhood (was a kind of treat 'cuz you could hear the ballgame almost continuously from all the front porch radios of all the sleeveless T-shirted guys as you passed by.) It was also a kind of uncomfortable treat because some guy or another always drove by and yelled out, "Hey, Joe Bright, need a lift?" Depending on my dad's answer, either, "Nah, we can walk," or "Yeah, sure, thanks, buddy," I might find myself scrunched in a back seat crammed with tool boxes and tackle boxes, and lots of miscellaneous stuff. But at least we had a ride to wherever we were headed, and although listening to grown men shooting the bull was not my idea of fun, at least we were riding in a car, and that was fun, for sure.

Cowboy Boots

I had just gotten new cowboy boots for my birthday. I was happy. I was ten years old. By the next afternoon, about 4 p.m., it had all changed. I heard a loud thud on our back porch. My father had fallen down, dead drunk, in plain potential view of our neighbors' open-screened windows. Total humiliation and sadness and anger simultaneously. Trying to drag him into the house, a man who outweighed me by 100 lbs or so, and with me being slightly hobbled by my non-broken-in-yet cowboy boots, was a formidable task. But I did it.

Nearly thirty years later, and drunk again, my dad called me on the phone. I had just heard, in an earlier call from a former student, that John Lennon had been killed. My dad knew nothing about the Lennon tragedy ... he had just called me to rant ... about what I cannot remember. But we spent the next twenty to thirty minutes alternately hanging up on each other, then calling back, then hanging up again. This was not a smooth father-son relationship.

TV, Beer Signs, and Calendars

He was an odd little neighbor kid. Smallish, sandy-haired with freckles, and kind of quiet, but he had special treasures in his old house. There was the magic of early television images for after-school fascination. The magnetism of that small screen meant that visiting suppers were gobbled while still watching TV from their living room floor. But the best images of all were the ones in the shadowy basement.

Down that creepy, dark staircase was his dad's man-cave type workshop. Its dusty old workbenches were lit by one hanging light bulb and three entire walls of blinking, flashing, electric beer signs. Scattered between those colorful signs were multiple calendars, of all sizes, with sexy "naked" women for each month! It was Magic-Land, like a night-time midway at a fair.

Tracking Phobias

"C'mon, you guys ... get me out of here! C'mon now, get me out," I yell over and over, with some semi-profane variations, and with increasing panic! I'm scrunched up, knees to chin, and trapped, between floors, in a half-finished dumbwaiter in its terribly narrow elevator shaft. This weird and scary scenario is happening in the partially constructed new Church Recreation/ Sunday School Center. My tortured distress is being met with much malicious delight by three or four of my sixth grade churchgoing buddies who have placed me in there and tied it off. God only knows why I agreed to get into the damn contraption to begin with ... some misplaced sense of a "being bad" adventure, I suppose. My demonic friends come and go, roaming the building for about 10 minutes before returning to finally end my claustrophobic suffering by hand cranking the chain to pull me up and out. Ahhh ... God ... space ... air ... I can stand up ... and breathe!

Many, many years later, my third, and hopefully, final wife, frequently asks me why I always push objects away from me on dining tables, whether at home or at restaurants ... like salt and pepper shakers, half-filled water glasses, sugar packet containers, etc. Never thought much about it 'til now. Just a goofy habit I'd supposed.

But, aha, perhaps the habit had a cause, a traumatic precedent even?   Childhood trauma.   Trapped in a claustrophobic dumbwaiter shaft!

Even Freud would laugh.

Disruption

Mechanical drawing class in eighth grade. It's the last period of the day. The classroom phone rings. The teacher takes a call ... listens and hangs up, saying nothing. He comes over to my drawing table. He says quietly that the office wants me to come there now. Have I done something wrong? He smiles reassuringly, but just indicates that I should go.

The long walk through the deserted, echoing hallway feels like some movie, where the guy is going to his execution. Turns out, it wasn't far from that. In the office was my mom, waiting to take me out of school a little early. She had something to tell me.

It was a sunny day ... the fresh air felt good after the "death walk" through the hallway. She said that we were going to the nearby ice cream store, where we could talk. So far, so good. But once there, and having ordered, she stunned me with the news that she had decided to get a divorce. She just couldn't take my dad's alcoholism any more. There was never any money for the family necessities because he would spend most of every paycheck at a bar before bringing the remainder home. It was just too hard for her to continue like that ... always trying to make do with nothing. She didn't mention the

15

loud arguing sessions, or that my dad screamed at her whenever she brought up his excessive drinking behavior to him, or the lack of money for groceries.

She had picked me up early so that she and we would not be at home when my dad was being served with the divorce papers by some court official. Oddly, I do not remember my little sister being with us. She must have also been in school. Hmmm...?

At any rate, we finally went home. My dad was there and furious! "How could you do this to me," he screamed. "I'll look like a fool! What will everybody think?" On and on he screamed. I was to find out only later that no one in our church had ever gotten a divorce before then. The Church was a powerful social force in our lives. My mother was brave to seek the divorce. She would be looked down upon a bit too. People in our church "just didn't do that." My father continued to shout ... he was banging his fist on the kitchen table. It felt violent. I was scared. I grabbed a paring knife from the sink, pointed it at him. And yelled myself, "Leave her alone! Stop shouting. Stop it , stop it," as I slowly followed him around the table, pointing the knife at him. Now my mother began to cry and tell me repeatedly to "put down the knife, put down the knife." I actually do not remember how all the frighteningness finally dissolved. But somehow it did.

I expect that my dad stomped out the door to a bar somewhere. Eventually, as it was said then, I became a "product of a broken home."

Guilt in a Shoe

"There, that feels better, doesn't it?" Uttered many years ago, with a persuasive and charmingly reassuring smile. The "victim" was a 12- or 13-year-old, very overweight, obviously poor, little girl with tattered shoes. She had come into the shoe store alone with a $5.00 bill crumpled up in her pudgy clenched hand. She wanted a pair of "those gold threaded girls' tennis shoes." Those shoes, with metallic gold threads woven into them cost $3.99 and were the rage of the young teenage girls at the time.

I measured her foot. It was big and wide. I went into the back room where the shoes were kept. There was only one pair of those shoes. They were not her size. I was a 19 year old college kid shoe salesman. I tried one on her slightly smaller right foot. Her toes were scrunched. She mustered all her courage and said, "I think these are maybe a little too tight. Do you have a bigger pair?" "Let me see," lied I. Back I went into the storeroom with that same pair of shoes. I proceeded to "stretch" them with some little wooden shoe-shaped insert tool that we used for just such a purpose. It never worked. Not really. But of course, I brought that same pair back out to the little heavyset girl, tried the one on her right foot again, leaned back on my stool, smiled, and uttered that infamous phrase, "There, that feels better, doesn't it?" She looked up, with a slightly confused and tortured look. She wanted those shoes. "Yes," she blurted out, and stuffed the $5.00 bill into my hand. They look nice, why don't you wear them outside, I said ... knowing that once they were worn on the street, they could not be returned. "Ok," she said. And up to the cash register we went. A sale! I had done my job. But clearly, at age 74 now, I have never forgotten that little girl. Who was I then?

The Nice Lady Nobody Asked To Dance

My mom was good to me. She was good to everyone. If somebody from the Church community was in the hospital, my mom was there. If there was a wake for someone who had died, my mom was there. If the Church needed someone to help in the kitchen with coffee after services, my mom was there. She was the Nice Lady.

Everyone liked her, she was so kind, but she had few close friends. Why? She was bright, pleasant enough looking, sincerely helpful, but she was shy ... and quiet, and not much fun perhaps, and she was divorced — unheard of in our parish at the time. At the many church, social club dances, she mostly sat on the sidelines and watched. Only two men ever asked her to dance. She would always tell me the next day about those one or two special dances that she had with one or both of those two fellows ... her only dances in an entire evening. Sometimes tears would appear in her eyes. Those two guys were my heroes.

II. BIGGER WORLDS

Route 66

I didn't have a Corvette convertible. I didn't have a Corvette. I didn't have a car. But I wanted to hit the road. It was the end of my freshman year at college, and I wanted to be like the two cool guys on the popular TV show, *Route 66*. They travelled the country, in a Corvette convertible, having adventures. "Me too," I thought. But no car. Back then, however, hitchhiking was still an acceptably safe and adventurous way to get about. There were not so many bad guys out there ... or at least not so much instant media to warn us, perpetually, about those who were. So, hitchhiking was going to be the vehicle of choice for me. I packed a small, old, beat-up, almost card-board-like suitcase of my mom's, slapped a big decal on it with my University's logo, and stuck out my thumb.

There were many adventures along the way. But the one that sticks with me mostly, even before reaching Route 66, was my ride and five days' worth of intrigue after being picked up in Nebraska somewhere by an ex-convict named Johnny and his wife named Flo. Johnny had just been out of prison for a few days, and had somehow obtained a beaten up old car that was chugging them both toward Colorado, where they "knew someone" on Denver's then famed skid row, Larimore Street, who could get them some jobs.

Johnny and Flo and I drove together for several days. We became friends. By the time we got to Denver and Larimore Street, which they knew well, we were like family ... maybe I was the kid they never had. They found us a couple of rooms in a seedy hotel, the only way to describe it. It was on a corner, and as that first evening sun went down, I watched through my dirty up-lifted window, in my hot stuffy room, with one overhanging bare light bulb, a corner sink, and a bathroom down the hall, as the girls of the night sauntered diagonally back and forth from corner to corner looking for trade. Fascinating.

The next day was the day to look for jobs. I had decided that having an adventure meant going with my new friends to get a job, stay in Denver for awhile, and see what would happen next. Now this is the just-like-a-movie part:

After walking a short distance in the distressed, dingy streets, we came to another derelict hotel. This was the place. We entered the grayish lobby area, which was occupied by a number of "bums" as we called them then, reclining in various prone and half-prone positions on wooden benches attached to all the walls, like an old train station or bus depot. Near the back of this large and hollow sounding room was a huge, heavy wooden counter, behind which was a very tall, almost scary looking man staring blankly ahead. As we approached he turned his gaze to us. Johnny showed him a piece of paper and asked to see someone. The tall man looked at the paper, then back to us, pulled some keys out of a drawer behind the counter, and nodded silently for us to follow him. We did. He led us to a formidable looking door, with no doorknob, at the absolute back of the lobby, inserted a key, swung the door open for us and stepped aside ... all in total silence.

As we peered into the doorway, all we could see in the absolute darkness beyond was the glow of a light somewhere at the bottom of what appeared to be a circular, spiraling staircase down into the void. Black curtains surrounded us as we made our way cautiously down into the shadowy depths. What to expect?

At the very bottom was another black curtain, behind which emanated the glow. Pushing it aside, Johnny stepped in first, revealing a gangster-looking guy with dark hair and moustache, wearing a slick looking pin-striped suit, and seated with his legs up on a massive, mahogany desk, an expensive piece of furniture, not at all fitting for the rest of the establishment. As this guy and Johnny exchanged subdued greetings and began to talk, the operation began to become clear to me. This was an "employment" office for down-and-out guys, who got a room in the hotel in exchange for working at menial temporary jobs, exchanging a significant percentage of their wages directly to the slick guy behind the massive desk, who was also the owner of this hotel. More conversation, and we were all given reference slips to a variety of jobs to which we were to report the next day. We, however, were not going to stay in that hotel, and were going to be able to keep the majority of our wages, other than giving some initial percentage to this guy. Johnny and Flo were going to be aids at a nursing home. I was going to be a dishwasher in a restaurant. Although I had worked for a semester in college, spraying out coffee bean bags and scouring hardened cauldrons of dried, crusted mash potatoes for an automatic food vending service, this hot, steamy, sweaty job washing dishes, after four or five days, did not seem to be the *Route 66* adventure that I had had in mind. At the end of the week, I regretfully said my good-byes to Johnny and Flo, planned a clever, I thought, non-hitchhiking way out of Colorado ... another story ... and left my skid row adventure without even collecting what was left of my wages. Still heading west.

Back to College, Show Biz, and Marriage

If you had somehow managed to become president of your high school graduating class, you might think that you'd start off with that same kind of success in college. Not necessarily true.

It sure wasn't the case for me. I floundered about a bit in my first year of college, doing more than OK with grades, going to football games with old high school friends, but not meeting many new friends, and not really feeling a part of the college scene. After that freshman year, I hitchhiked to California. It was a grand adventure. While I was gone, I received what turned out to be a full four-year scholarship. So I came back. Then I took a theatre class. I was intrigued and captivated. I took another, then another, and another. I'd found a new "home." There were people I could relate to ... and be amused by ... and there was the thrill of creativity. There were also a lot of bright, attractive women. Eventually, there was even a wife. How hard is it to fall in love with a lovely, fine actress, who had actually played Juliet? And, if she'd have you, why not get married to her as well? Seemed like the smart thing to do! We did it. We figured that somehow we would manage to be in plays together, maybe even film or TV, be adventurous travelers, and have a happy and fulfilling creative life. Parts of all of that came true.

A Showboat to Germany

You can't take an old fashioned, paddle-wheel showboat across the ocean to Germany. But something just as unimaginable happened to me on a USO show tour of what was then West Germany ... the show having originated on an authentic, river based showboat in the USA. The show was a famous old Melodrama from the 19th century. I played the hero.

We played military bases all over Western Germany for a six week period in the mid 1960s. We were a youngish USO Show, college acting troupe in our early-to-late 20s. Mostly middle class, and as Midwestern as could be. There were two exceptions, two "older guys" in their mid-to-late 30s. They were former professional actors who had gone back to graduate school, so they could eventually get "real jobs" as college teachers. They were both originally from the East Coast, and they were both Jewish.

The tour was filled with wonders, but the most powerful of all was a sightseeing tour on one of our few days off. We rode our tour bus to Dachau! A former German concentration camp, where thousands of Jews had been imprisoned and killed. It was now preserved as a kind of memorial. When we arrived, our two Jewish colleagues both refused to get off the bus. They said they would wait for us on the bus. They were not even stepping on that ground. Powerful personal statements. I'm not at all sure that the rest of us really understood the profundity of that choice at the time.

When we disembarked from the bus, we were guided to witness many things. All eerily motionless now, but with their unthinkable horrors still hanging oppressively in the air.

Near the end of the tour, we were taken to a small museum-like building, which had a number of photos and other displays in a variety of frames and glass cases, all of which I viewed silently and reflectively. Until. Until I saw one rather small framed, under-glass photo, maybe 8 by 10 inches in size. It was a simple enough picture ... just three uniformed men facing front and smiling. But as I looked closely, it caused me to gasp, both audibly and in my heart. The three men were Hitler, Goering and I believe Goebbels. They were smiling broadly. Somehow, the eyes of each of them had been scratched out, leaving only pinpoint sized, glaringly white, empty holes. There was some handwriting in French beneath the disturbing image of the three men. I was able to translate it well enough to realize that it said, "They are smiling. Millions of others are weeping still." It was a stomach punch to the soul. We soon got back on our bus, with our two Jewish friends, and all was silent for a long time.

My First Pre-Wedding Eve

At the traditional wedding rehearsal dinner, where both families meet, often for the very first time, a major bummer happens.

I arrive early at my mother's small, modest house to help set up the table for dinner, etc. This will be an anxiety-producing, one-time-only dining experience, with such components as a probable arrival of a possibly drunken father, a well-to-do, teetotaling, perfectionist, orthodontist father-in-law, a pleasant but prim and proper, as they say, mother-in-law, and a ... wait, what's that on the buffet? As I begin to reach for the glass door behind which is the "good china," I spot a standing-on-edge envelope, leaning against some knickknack or other.

It's from The Draft Board! "What's this, Mom?" "Oh, I didn't want you to see that," she replies. "Then why the hell did you leave it standing up on the buffet," I say to myself. What can this be? I'm safely secure on a graduate-student deferment from the military, I think. The contents reveal that I have been reclassified 1-A, and am to report for my physical on such and such a day! I'm in shock. Everything is blurry. How can this be? My stomach is now in knots and my hands are sweating. "But I'm getting married TOMORROW," my brain screams. From that moment of angst, and throughout the foggy, disastrous-as-predicted-dinner, throughout the following hazy wedding rehearsal at the church, and through the actual wedding itself, part of me is not even there. I'm mentally absent, but smiling appropriately, and saying all the right things to all the right people, I guess.

Finally, we're married. The reception is, for me, a drunken one. "I'm going to Viet Nam," is all that I can think. I get really drunk, on the cheap Spanish wine my teetotaling father-in-law has dutifully provided. Because my now wife and I are still in grad school, we have classes on Monday morning, so no honeymoon has been planned. Good thing.

Our wedding night, at a fairly classy local hotel is also a disaster. There would be no point to being in Tahiti for such a disappointing evening. Needless to say, I was still drunk from the reception, and in a bad mood, and my poor dear bride was left hurt and wondering what the hell was going on? I had decided not to wreck our wedding, and wedding night, by sharing the destructive Draft Board news. I figured I'd wait until Monday morning when I could get some actual official answers as to the "why" of this attempted government sabotage of my marriage and my life.

Sure enough, bright and early Monday morning, following a horribly hung-over Sunday, and a now probably confused young wife thinking, "Who the hell did I marry, and why?" I got the ridiculous answer to my three-day trauma. Turns out that although I had paid my tuition for the next semester before the deadline, it had not been recorded until the next day, past the deadline, which had triggered an automatic government/draft board rejection of my student deferment status, and I had been reclassified 1-A! It was all a mistake!!!

Thank you God! But damn the bastards who caused it, and wrecked my wedding and my life for 40 tortuous hours! But still, it brought a great smile and many sighs of release and relief ... and some much needed explanations to my dear puzzled wife.

A Bumpy Start

After fifty some years of multiple relationships and marriages I am still trying to learn, apparently, how to "stop telling women what to do." I think that I am merely expressing concern and making suggestions when women seem to be having difficulty making a decision. That does not appear to be their perception of such situations. I know now, at age seventy-almost-four that it is un-cool to give un-solicited advice. Yet I can't seem to stop myself ... try as I may.

So, OK, many years ago, my first wife and I are sitting up in bed reading our lines to each other. We are both young actors at a big professional theatre in the Midwest, and are fairly newly wedded. We are each understudying roles of two lovers in the same romantic scene together. Oh, oh. In my youthful naiveté, and smart-assed-ness, I blurt out, after one of her line readings, "Are you really going to say it like that?" Oops! Was that it? A turning point? The beginning of the end perhaps? Although the marriage lasted for four more mostly good but up-and-down years, the downward trajectory may have begun. The damage, as they say, had been done, and the decline of the marriage was probably inevitable. "Never tell another actor what to do, or how to say a line." That's a theatre

"no-no" (but one which I had obviously not yet learned)—
and a special kind of "no-no" when said to a talented
actress/wife.

Connections with Grandma

Hollywood beckons. After several years of working as professional actors, and enduring the arctic-like winters of our hometown Minneapolis, my first not-yet-ex-wife and I decide that it is time to head to warmer climes, fame and fortune. California here we come! But before we leave, it's a "must" to visit my maternal grandmother in her nursing home.

On a still-winter afternoon, my not-yet-ex, my mom, and I all bundle up to drive over and say goodbye to Grandma. As we peer tentatively around the corner to the open door of Grandma's room, we are wondering how we will find her to be. The answer is even more than delightfully profound.

As we enter her room, with me leading the way, Grandma is sitting in a rocking chair in a corner by a window. I start off with, "Hi, Grandma, how are you?" Grandma looks up, smiles, and begins to rise. As she slowly crosses the room diagonally toward her bed, she says, "Well, when I'm standing up, I don't know anything." Then, gradually lowering herself onto her bed, she says, "but when I'm lying down, I know everything." My mom, my not-yet-ex, and I all take turns dropping our jaws and looking at each other. What did Grandma just say? Did we hear her right? My mother blurts out, "No, Grandma, you mean it the other way around." Grandma just smiles in silence. My not-yet-ex and I, who believe ourselves to be hip to all things cosmic, look at each other with deep knowing glances. Wow, no, Grandma got that right! Isn't she cool!

Much small talk later, we all hug our goodbyes a number of times, and head off into the cold. With a lot of love in our hearts. On our way to California.

III. EVEN BIGGER WORLDS

Hollywood

So, my first not-yet-ex-wife and I arrive in L.A., via a brief two week stay in San Francisco. We find a small apartment just two blocks off Hollywood Boulevard. We're actors. It'll do.

Lots of stuff happens. Taxi and pizza delivery jobs for me. Waitress jobs for her. Mime classes for me. Agent-seeking efforts for her. Psychic and Spiritual encounters for us both. Our minds have been opened. After all, we're in California. It's the early '70s, when anything is possible ... and everything is cool.

Cats in a Bag

Psychics, eh? "I see a tall, dark stranger in your future, and lots of money." If this is the extent of your encounters with psychics, either personally or in the movies, you might want to explore the phenomenon a little further ... just for fun, of course.

Back in my hippie days in California, when I was pretty open to anything, I was studying some eastern religious teachers, and was referred to an elderly woman who was a devotee of a particularly well-known and internationally respected spiritual master. The elderly woman passed along the teachings of this famous spiritual teacher. The woman was also a psychic. She attempted to pass along those skills as well. Her theory was that everyone had psychic abilities, but that they were not open enough to be in touch with them. It was basic intuition, she said, only at a higher level. That made some sense. When she offered to teach classes to help us, who regularly attended her Sunday spiritual sessions, to discover those psychic abilities individually, I was definitely intrigued, and signed up.

The idea, we were told, would be to have two separate classes, divided by gender, so as to have less possible sexual energies barring the transmission of pure psychic vibrations. That seemed a little weird, but also made a kind of sense, given the somewhat bizarre concept of psychic-ness to begin with. Our classes started, one evening a week, with about 10 curious male would-be-psychic adepts. For the first several weeks we did various yoga exercises to get in touch with our more relaxed higher consciousnesses. In about the third week, as I recall, we began some preliminary psychic exercises. That's when the fun began. Interesting mini-events began to occur.

Were they real or merely an odd coincidence? As we sat on the floor in a circle in our teacher's living room, we were asked to meditate for a few moments, and then to just open our minds to anything that might occur, particularly images. Then, no matter how strange the thoughts or images might be, we would share them with the group. Just to trust and to see what might come forth, was the idea. This was a little scary. I remember thinking, "What if I don't get any images? I'll look and feel stupid." So much for my sense of open, centered-being-ness. But, whew, I got an image. I saw a rifle standing on end in a broom closet. Not too weird. When my turn came round, I shared that. One of the guys said that in his family's house, his dad had just such a setup. I was congratulated with having had a possible mini-psychic experience. One more round was coming up. Our teacher was sitting right next to me. I was feeling pretty cool. I figured I would focus mentally on her a bit, since she was probably emitting the strongest vibrations. We breathed and meditated again for a time, and then were asked to begin sharing our experiences. Uh, oh. This time I had gotten a really weird image. I didn't have the centeredness to share that one. My "cool" was gone. I didn't want to seem foolish. So we went around the room, not everyone had something to say this time, and that was apparently OK. I kept my mouth shut. Our teacher began to wrap things up, but stopped and asked, "Does anyone have anything else they would like to say?" I'm calmly sitting, not about to unzip my lips. Across from me in the circle and a little to my right is another hippie-esque young man with funny hair, and brightly shining, very clear eyes. He smiles gently at me, points and says, "He does." All turn to look at me. My heart races. "Well, do you?" asks the teacher. There's no getting away from it now. I'm not going to lie, not in a spiritual class.

I swallow. I begin with a kind of stammer, "Does ... does anyone here ... anyone here ... anyone have any kind of ... kind of ... connection to putting a cat in a brown bag?" There. Done. I've said it. Immediately, my teacher, seated on the floor next to me, lets out a kind of shriek, and rolls down onto her back. The room seems to stop breathing. She pushes herself up with her elbows, back into her yoga-like seated position, while exclaiming surprisedly, "My God, I haven't thought of that in 60 years!" We all stare at her. What? What? She begins to explain.

"You all know that I was born in England. We used to live on a peninsula-like area, right near the ocean. Our long back yard ended at a kind of bog, which was often surrounded by mist or fog. At one point when I was very young ... maybe about five or six years old ... we heard some strange animal-like cries from the back yard for several nights in a row. On the third night when the cries sounded again, my father took a flashlight and went out back in the yard to see what it was. We waited awhile, then cautiously followed him out. What I saw was a bunch of little scrawny kittens that my father said were dying of mange. He was putting them all in a brown burlap sack to drown them and put them out of their misery! I did my best to put that out of my mind ... and I have not thought of that again over these past 60 years ... 'til just now."

Make of it what you will.

Magic, Mime and a Mystical Religion

It may be viewed as un-cool now, but mime has always seemed magical to me. As a kid watching a famous French mime on TV, I was always delightfully captivated. I felt that I could actually see that imaginary ladder he was climbing, and the invisible walls of the room closing in on him. How could he do that? Later, I felt the same way about a famous singer's moonwalk dance moves, and NBA basketball players' reverse dunks while taking off into the air from beyond the free-throw line. How could any of them do that? It all seemed like magic.

So, I find myself in LA, pursuing a professional acting career and taking a mime class. Why mime and not an acting for the camera class? Who knows now? I'm guessing that a mime class taught by a semi-starving mime, was probably cheaper. At any rate, the guy teaching the mime class had written a mime book.

I bought it. On the back inside flap, he gave his bio, which casually mentioned a mysterious spiritual discipline that he had stumbled upon in his travels, the practice of which "got you high." No drugs, but "high." Well, that was intriguing to me! One day, after class, I got brave and asked him about it. It couldn't be verbally explained he said, but if I was genuinely interested, he would tell me how to attend a session, and I could experience it for myself. You bet. So arrangements were made. It was all very secretive, without feeling deceptive in any way.

OK. Suffice it to say, that after meeting one evening at the pre-arranged time and place, a modern and attractive one story building somewhere in the Valley, and being introduced by my mime teacher to a number of other pleasant people, the oddness of it all began. I'm asked to sit in a small closet, with the lights off, and to "just listen and take in" whatever I hear happening in the next room, but which I cannot see. Hmmm. All right. I'm game. It'll take about an hour I'm told. Just relax and absorb. After a few minutes, alone in my little darkened closet, I hear people's footsteps shuffling into some space next door, which must be carpeted from the sound of it. Then some sense of group movement begins to happen. They must be walking about in some pattern in that room. Next , some sounds of a kind of chanting occurs, but not by everyone and not in unison. Just sporadically. Several voices are soaringly beautiful, while others are more like small moans which are punctuated by a few sudden shouts or screams of apparent mental suffering. Occasionally, the flowing sound of the movement is interrupted by a rapid shuffling of feet, like someone is darting across the room.

That's usually when the brief screams are heard. What the hell is happening in there? My brain is racing. I can't help trying to visualize it, while simultaneously trying to stay relaxed and calm and "in the moment." As time goes by, the sounds become more and more familiar, and I am able to relax and quiet my mind. Mostly, I am able to "zone out," as we used to say, and just "absorb." The next thing I know, the strange sounds and floor movement begin to slow down. Then stop. People are leaving that room. A few normal, conversational voices grow nearer to me. There is a gentle knock on my closet door, and then it opens. Light filters in from the hall, and one of the men quietly asks me how I'm feeling. I stand slowly, and discover that I am feeling pleasantly stoned. Really. Just like having smoked some good weed. Hmmm. Well. I guess I may need to explore this ritual a little further. More magic.

The Big Trip

I moved from Hollywood to New York to "drop acid." It was to be a temporary move because my first not-yet-ex-wife was keeping our apartment in LA. We were still married, and planning to stay that way. My other reason for going to NY was to see if my career pursuit really needed to be live theatre acting, rather than film acting. The mission to take acid for the first time was part of my calling to "try everything" in life, so that I could be a better actor, and to feel that I was experiencing everything that life had to offer.

At the time, the very early '70s, people said that in taking LSD initially, you should do it with someone you love and trust, who had already had experience with the drug. I had two good friends there, a husband and wife team whom I knew from grad school, and with whom I shared those love and trust feelings. They had also both taken acid many times.

My friends had a huge loft in the Chelsea area. I got to live with them rent free until I could find my own place. They had many talented and fascinating friends who often stopped by. It was all very cool!

NYC is a special place. I missed my wife, but I was certainly living fully. But, the day to take the LSD trip wasn't materializing. I asked about it often, but not too often. My friends were just too busy with their own crazy, daily NY lives.

Then, finally, after several weeks, on a gorgeous, sunny Sunday, my friends decided it was time. I was excited. I tried to stay calm. Breakfast came and went. Time ticked slowly by. About noon I was shown a little orange pellet, slightly smaller than a grain of rice. Could this be it! All the consciousness raising power I had heard so much about? Had thought about so often? In just this little pill?

Yep, that was it. A preparatory gulp, and then down the hatch. We're off!

Now, I'm the only one tripping that day, as I recall. My two friends, and a couple of their friends, were just going to act as my guides. It would take a little while for it to come on, I was told. But it wasn't long at all. Soon, I was flying! The sky was never so blue. The sun bouncing off the Hudson River, where we had walked, was never so bright. My mind was experiencing anything and everything simultaneously! We left the river after awhile and headed back across town, past the East Village, towards NYU. Washington Square felt like a zoo. Fellow strange looking hippie types to begin with, had an even more Fellini-esque quality now under the influence of the magic potion. I was really tripping!

But, suddenly, for no apparent reason, I got scared. Then, a bit paranoid. I didn't feel that I should say anything to the others, so as not to bum them out. I, of course, should have. That's why they were there. Instead, I began pretending that all was fine. And worse, I told them that I wanted to go off on my own. Big mistake. They all asked me to stick with them, and that it might be good to do so, but I felt that I had to get away, and be on my own. So I left. I had their assurances that all would be fine, and that they would see me later back at the loft. Well, it didn't happen that way!

So I'm heading back toward the safety of the loft in the West Village, but I'm feeling pretty out of control. I need a little stabilizer, I think. I'm passing a dinky sidewalk bar ... but you have to go down three or four steps to enter. Somehow I manage to order a straight shot of whiskey, then another and another ... I don't think that I talked with anyone, just looked down at my glass, or out onto the sunny sidewalk, which was pretty much at eye level. Just saw legs going by. Pretty Surreal.

Next thing I knew I was back inside the loft. No one else was back yet. I was alone. I needed some soothing music for companionship. I found Cat Steven's album *Tea for the Tillerman* in a pile of LP's and put it on the phonograph, with the arm of the machine off to the side, which meant that the record would simply play over and over and over.

That's what it did … until about 5 a.m. the next morning, with me just lying, semi-propped up on a kind of couch, listening to those lyrics, in a kind of haze, repeating themselves again and again. No one of my group of friends ever returned that night. Can't even remember what they told me when they returned mid morning. They had probably gone to someone else's pad to hang out, and simply crashed there. I had come down from the acid sometime in the very early morning, but chose to just lie where I safely was, until someone returned. When they finally did return, the healing/hauntingly beautiful Cat Steven's music was still playing. It's burned into my brain … and I love that record even today!

Changes ... and Five Amazing Days

Time passes. Four years of goofy living situations later, after living with my wife in Los Angeles for six months, living alone in NYC for three months to pursue stage acting, then returning to LA for an intoxicant influenced, whirlwind decision to get divorced, I now find myself being driven north to relocate to the Bay Area. I was in NY on Friday, LA on Saturday, playing on the beach in Malibu on Sunday, and by Monday night I'm living as a soon-to-be single man, in exciting and stunningly beautiful San Francisco. By Tuesday evening I was sleeping on the floor of my new hilltop studio apartment in The City by the Bay. Talk about a quick turn-around ... a big time state of shock and then some ... but ahhhh ... San Francisco.

The San Francisco Mystery Woman

She showed up in my mind before we ever met. The archetype of the exotic, sexy African-American goddess. She thought of herself that way, too ... Egyptian goddess that is. She was a poet. A street savvy, nineteen-year-old waif, admiring of Rimbaud, and writing her own odes to madness.

She materialized in a bar on a chilling, foggy night in North Beach ... sitting alone at a table, wrapped regally in her black velvet cloak. She looked at my friend and me with an aloof gaze, but one which said "I'm here, if you dare." My friend spoke to her. She joined us at our table. We bought her a drink, and were mesmerized by her eyes, and her beauty. I recall nothing of the conversation, nor really when she left. She seemed like a dream. Then, three days later, she materialized again. I was at work. I glanced up and there she was in a corner of the store, staring at me. This time she smiled. A strangely involved journey together began.

Not the Best Time to Start a Theatre

When you are newly divorced, in shock, relocated, and without any money to speak of, the obvious thing to do is start a theatre. With a fellow I had met when my now-first "ex" and I originally came to San Francisco, I co-started an Actors' Equity union-approved Showcase Theatre. A first such theatre in San Francisco! We created a series of off-beat plays that got good advance publicity, were received quite well by critics, but which drew little or no audiences.

Of course this was exacerbated by the fact that one of our plays was an intense prison drama written by an ex-convict from San Quentin Penitentiary, who just happened to also be a member of Mensa, supposedly. The play was produced by us at a time when the "Zebra Killings" were occurring on the streets of San Francisco. These killings were the random shootings of whites by blacks ... there had been ten or eleven deaths already. A climate of fear was everywhere.

Unfortunately, all of our advance attempts at attention-getting publicity photos had gone out to the press showing pictures of prison guards being held at knifepoint by black convicts, the play having been based on an actual prison riot that had occurred in San Quentin. The people of San Francisco were afraid to leave their houses and apartments to go out even for groceries, let alone to see a play about black prisoners committing potential violence! Too bad for our little theatre adventure ... it was almost funny. And like all good comedy, one of the secrets is timing!

Dead Horse Pass

I had never backpacked in the wilderness in my life. When the opportunity arose to go on a 33 day survival trip, it seemed to my mid-1970s hippie mind, like the logical adventure to try.

Learning how to swing an 80 lb. back pack and frame, including 20 lbs. of food, up and over and onto my back was only the beginning of the challenge. At the time, I only weighed 128 lbs, and was 5 feet 8 inches tall. I had just completed a year of intense karate training, so I was in great shape, but it was far from a rugged and burly mountaineer's body ... or a mountaineer's mind.

A guiding principle of the survival trek was to leave nature undisturbed, as we had found it. So, all bodily waste had to be buried in a hole carefully dug and then recovered with the original pieces of earth. A total drag, but a noble endeavor. Well, on a certain fortunately starry night, I was suddenly afflicted with a severe and ongoing stomach upset, requiring its total evacuation ... hourly!

The routine: put on my boots in the dark, crawl out of the tent, find a spot near no trees (we were not allowed to cut through any roots while digging our individual latrines), dig the hole placing each piece of earth in a row along side so it could be easily replaced in sequence, pull down my pants and squat over the hole as best I can to "do my business" of mostly uncontrollable diarrhea (apologies for this gross-out but that's the facts) and then reverse and repeat this entire sequence of actions five or six times during the long tortuous night! All the while knowing and dreading that our usual seven to ten mile daily trek the next day was scheduled to begin with a very narrow, winding climb over something called Dead Horse Pass! This was a nightmare of a night, to say the least, but it wasn't a nightmare, it was real. You couldn't make this stuff up!

Finally, my agonizing stomach discomfort subsided. The requisite venturing forth in the dark ended only an hour or two before the sun began to rise. I was mercifully granted this brief time to sleep. But, we were awakened soon to begin our journey up and over Dead Horse Pass! In my nearly sleepless and extremely weakened condition, the winding ascent on a two foot wide trail at about 10,000 feet elevation, using my ice ax as a cane as I overlooked the drop-off below, was not my idea of a heroic outdoor adventure. But when the stressful day finally ended, and I had made it successfully to our next camp site, I was exhausted and shaky, but was damned proud of myself! And by the end of this 33 day survival trip in the wilderness, with the last four days being in groups of only four, and without food, we were all damned proud!

The trip culminated in a wonderfully drunken party at a local bar in the town where the trip had begun and ended. But as positive as the entire experience had been, and all the wilderness experience I had acquired, and even enjoyed, "learning how to redefine our definition of fun," I've never been backpacking again.

Providing a New and Enriching Experience

Working as a teacher with an inner city kid in an inner city junior high school, can be a rewarding experience ... or not. My goal was to show a kid with some promise, that there was another kind of life that could be lived, by visiting a high-end hotel in a wealthy area high above much of the city. We took a two person field trip ... can't imagine now how I pulled that off. I'm pretty sure that it was a regular school day. But, our school was a special alternative school, the last stop before the city-wide detention center for kids who had been kicked out of their regular school(s) ... so we had the ability as alternative education teachers to bend the rules somewhat and be creative in our attempts to help the "troubled youth" who comprised our school's entire populace.

Wandering the halls of the ultra classy Fairmont Hotel in San Francisco with my junior high school juvenile delinquent, but likeable, early teenager was an iffy experience at best. The kid was wearing a black "hoodie," 40 years before they were called hoodies. We called them "sweat jackets" back then. I still do. I was wearing a jean jacket, a rolled orange bandana headband, and some beads around my neck.

It's a wonder that we were not followed by security

from the moment we entered the hotel. Maybe we were ... initially. Clearly, as it turned out, we were not followed throughout our wanderings within the breath-taking chandeliered lobby, hallways, and ballrooms. How do I know? Because when I figured that I had awed my student sufficiently, and it was time for our leave-taking, on the way out the door, my young friend proudly showed me the entire setting of silverware, cloth napkin wrapped, that he had somehow smoothly pilfered, without my even noticing, from our little visit to an "enriching experience" in another world.

Grandma, Revisited

San Francisco is an amazing place to be in the early '70s, but, it seems time for my first return visit to Minneapolis to visit my family and friends.

Family, of course, would include, Mom, Dad, and Grandma. Many uncles and aunts too. On the day of my departure for the Twin Cities, I am wondering why I am feeling a need to go now. It's March but it's still going to be cold there. I get a sudden intuitive flash, and tell my girlfriend at the time that my Grandma is going to pass away while I'm there. She's waiting for me to come back, so that I can help the family, which is a highly sensitive one, through the ordeal of her death. My girlfriend smiles and reassures me that all will be fine.

I'm home for three days. Staying in my old room at my mother's house. I've seen my mom and a few friends so far, but that's it. I'm sleeping in a little late. It's about 8:15 a.m., and I am awakened by the phone ringing downstairs. An odd time for a call. Something's up. I rush down to the phone, and manage to get there in time to pick up the receiver and hear my mother's strange sounding voice. "They just called and told me Grandma has just died. She's at the hospital. Can you come here to my work, pick me up, and take me there?" "Whew. Sure. OK. I'll be there as soon as I can … about a half hour."

Some semi-frantic driving, much calming of Mom, and an arrival at the hospital. For some unexplained reason, grandma has been left in a hallway on a gurney, and with a sheet over her body and face. We are told we can lift the sheet to look at her, and spend as much time there as we wish. My mom continues to cry … she is very emotional and often cries … but this is different. We pull back the sheet from her face. Grandma looks serene. I have no idea of how long we are there … just looking … with tears. My mom kisses her mom. I kiss Grandma too. I put the sheet back over her face. I hug my mom. We talk briefly with a nurse. We leave. Grandma and I have reconnected. She was a very special woman.

Saved by a Match

I'm acting in a play about a somewhat fictionalized version of an actual major prison riot near San Francisco. My character is named "Shitty Smitty," an old coot convict who burned down a kids' school years ago, and who rubs human feces on himself to prevent being sexually harassed by other convicts. The play is written by an ex-convict who was actually in the prison at the time of the riot. He has a genius level IQ and says he is a member of Mensa. He was in prison for over 20 years, multiple times, for multiple armed robberies. Go figure.

Side note, on stage combat — training techniques for actors in order to fight safely on stage: A key idea for such rough-stuff is called "energy pull-back." Basically, whether it's a slap, a punch, or a kick toward another actor, you mentally and physically must avoid making actual contact, and "pull back" the attacking energy, even as you are physically sending it forward. This, did I mention, is a key idea. Without this concept and training, an actor in the heat of emotion can easily lose control and injure a fellow actor/opponent. Problem. In this particular play, there are lots of actors without this training.

In the play, Shitty Smitty, wanders the prison yard

67

feeding popcorn to the pigeons. But, he's a "stool pigeon," and mixes tiny, crumpled-up pieces of white paper with the popcorn, giving tip-off notes to the guards.

As the actor playing Shitty Smitty, I sometimes enjoy nibbling on the popcorn backstage ... an acting no-no. Never eat the props. But what the hell, my character is a child-murdering old bastard. I'm embodying him. Why would I follow some silly rules against prop-eating? But I digress.

In one scene in the play, Smitty, tips off the guards to the forthcoming escape plans which will later result in the riot. But, good old Shitty Smitty is soon caught by the leader of the rebel convicts, the hero of the play, and Smitty is threatened, to force him to confess to whatever secret information he has been passing along. The rebel leader and another young convict grab me, as Shitty Smitty, bend me backwards over a bench in the yard, and yank a belt tightly around my neck to torture me into talking. The younger convict is also directed to light a wooden match near Smitty's face, threatening to burn him/me.

One night, during an actual performance, the lack of stage combat training rears its ugly head ... big time! The rebel convict is a big man. Strong. He's yelling at me. He's emotional. He pulls too hard on the belt, choking me. I black out onstage! I'm fully out, I later discover, for about 10-15 seconds. The other two actors are panicked and frozen in place. The young one, knowing nothing else to do, goes ahead with his torturing bit of lighting the match in my face. The sulphur from that striking of the match goes right up my nose, like a kind of smelling salt action, and I am startled awake, both groggy and stunned. What? What's going on? Oh my god, look at their faces! They are freaked out. Geezuz! They must have choked me out. Then someone, me or one of them, manages to get out some line of dialogue, and we are somehow able to continue with the play ... the audience never knowing what has actually happened ... thinking it's all part of the play.

I'm thinking, "thank god" for the match!

Old Ladies and Old Men

Male and Female relationships in the semi-misnamed 1960s. "Hippies, Freaks ... Weird ... Far Out ... the Sexual Revolution." Nobody got married, but it seemed like everyone slept together. It was cool, man. And if you ever wanted an ongoing sexual partner, you had "your old lady," or "your old man." In the '60s nobody was ever old. "Forever Young" was the rule of the day.

The Golden Flower

I'm sitting on the ground beside a pretty little lake in Golden Gate Park on a beautiful sunny day in San Francisco. How can I be so totally depressed? An acid trip going awry! I can't even make myself stand up to go home.

At some point in my hazy confusion I happen to look down. I spot at my feet a single dandelion. I look at it. Then I look deeper. Then deeper still.

Now I'm consumed by it. I'm inside the flower. I'm one with the flower. Everything is Golden. I relax. I smile.

I stand up. I look up at the beautiful blue sky. I smile more. I'm able to walk to the bus and head home.

Some years later, as I'm recalling this story to friends, it occurs to me that my total immersion into the golden dandelion in the park had become a perfect metaphor for conquering depression. That Golden Flower could and did become, in both my life and my teaching, a symbol for any uplifting activity that we know makes us feel good whenever we choose to absorb ourselves in it, like playing our favorite up-beat music, taking a walk outside, or talking to a good friend. However, at the time, it was just part of a bad acid trip ... that got magically better because I had looked at the Golden Flower.

Madman

He probably saved my life. He was an ironworker. Up there walking on steel beams, creating skyscrapers. Hard to imagine. I never saw him at work. I have a fear of heights.

He was a powerful, physical man. He had a tremendous IQ, and had been a member of some form of the Communist Party in London early on, then became a strong union advocate as a steel worker in San Francisco. Later in life he studied and became an experimental, abstract artist, exploring shape and texture, and finally the use of sculpted, painted steel. Stunning work. An amazing guy. Oh, and he always drank a lot!

I did too. After one particularly devastating drinking/stoned, injury-causing episode on that rented cable car Christmas caroling party, this friend, who had been there, called me the next day. In my almost suicidal, remorseful and humiliated state of mind, I almost ignored the long-ringing phone. He had sensed my emotional state, and with great, though out-of-the-box wisdom, told me he was coming over to take me out to shoot pool and drink a few beers. I protested, but he over-rode me, and showed up soon at my door. Never mentioning the nightmare night of yesterday, and while beating me probably in eight ball, he concluded our fairly silent pool-playing by saying that I might want to consider not drinking or taking drugs for one month, just to see if I could do it. No judgment … no admonitions … just this challenge to see what I would discover. I did as he said. I discovered a lot. No puritan still, I've been on a far better path ever since. My friend has become a brilliant, madman artist recluse in a quaint little town in Oregon somewhere. He communicates with me via only five or six usually puzzling words in the subject line of a once or twice per year belated email reply to my requests for contact. An unforgettable guy. I wish him well.

That Pivotal Day

Some 40 years later, it really does seem like only a bad dream, an amusing recall of a bad dream ... about being down and out.

It was an unseasonably hot, sunny autumn day for the Bay Area. The fun and freedom of my hippie life was melting away in the heat with me. I had sunken low enough financially that I now found myself hiking up and down some minor hills somewhere in the East Bay carrying two 20-lb. sacks of handbills hung over my front and over my back, advertising god knows what. We were delivering them somewhere in a kind of subdivision area, which makes no sense if you are familiar with the East Bay. We had arrived there from the skid-row part of downtown San Francisco, in the back of a stiflingly enclosed black panel truck. "We," being the five other down-and-outer-handbill-distributors like myself. Only bad breath, body odor, and the smell of sweating out liquor was in the humid air in the back of that truck.

When we arrived at our destination, we were given specific directions as to where to go and how to fulfill our noble task, positioning only one handbill in each door, in just such and such a folded manner. The truck would pick us up again in four hours. We would then have some kind of half hour lunch break (how, since we had no money? Had we been told to bring a lunch?) and then that black, hearse-like vehicle would take us onward to a new location for the later afternoon.

After seeming days of trudging from door to door, sweating profusely from my own probable over-consumption of wine from the night before (and the many nights before that), I began to gain some insights … fuzzy insights, but nonetheless, insights.   I had already completed 10 years of college! Was this a suitable activity for someone who should probably be a college professor, rather than a handbill carrier?   Perhaps not.   Maybe I should take a re-look at my lifestyle. Maybe I could live a more fulfilling life, one in which I could actually earn a living. What might that be like? If I had just spent five bohemian years dropping out, maybe I could find a way to drop back in?   How would I go about it, became the question that occupied my sweating brain for the next 50-100 handbills.

Suddenly, the answer came to me! Return to my home town, Minneapolis! There, people would still know me, and might remember the prior successful, actor-grad-student-teacher me. I could catch a break and get re-started in a better life. It made some kind of sense to me, out there in the heat of nowhere-land. I vowed at that very moment to make a change, even if it meant leaving behind my beloved San Francisco, where I had adventured for the last five years. With my brain abuzz through the haze, I plotted my way out. When the hearse-like truck finally arrived to move us to a new locale, I boldly told the two men in charge that "I was through!" I returned their two sacks with the remaining handbills inside, turned on my heel, as they say, and strode off toward the hazy view of the San Francisco skyline miles off in the distance beyond the Bay Bridge.

I walked all the way, as I recall. But did I really do that? It seems insane. My memory says yes, but I can't fully imagine it. Looking up some facts, the answer is apparently no. The Bridge was never walkable, until it's current renovation. So who knows how I got across it? I had no money for transportation. Perhaps I hitchhiked. Perhaps I borrowed or begged some money for a TransBay bus ride, maybe I somehow even had a bus pass. In any case, I walked a lonnng way from my point of declaration of liberty from handbills. I finally, somehow, got to the dreary office from which we had departed many hours earlier, demanded and received my pay for the half day, which came to about $6.50 after taxes. Still, I felt good. Something had changed. Something new was going to happen. It would be better.

Tai Chi, a Long and Winding Road

I used to be a skinny little guy. Now I'm a stocky little guy. As a kid, whenever I saw those ads about "Don't let a bully on the beach kick sand in your face," I wanted to be a big strong guy! I worked hard to become a pretty good athlete.

But if you were still basically "little," and wanted to kick sand back at the bully, you probably had to become a martial artist. In my late 20s, I studied Karate three and four times a week for a year. I got into great physical shape, and it was good for my confidence, but it wasn't ultimately right for me. Then I heard about Tai Chi. It sounded like a better fit. No force against force, but yielding to your opponent's force and using it against him. Sounded good to me.

Finding a good tai chi teacher was an intriguing adventure. In San Francisco there was no shortage of Asian Martial Arts teachers. How to find the right one?

After dabbling in it for months, as I vagabonded through two different cities, in two different states, I found just the teacher for me, and his tai chi studio turned out to be just one mile from my San Francisco apartment. Seemed like fate, and this man could do things that were seemingly impossible.

I walked over to his tai chi school on another beautiful, sunny, San Francisco afternoon. I climbed up the narrow steps to his second floor studio, peeked in, saw no one in the big sunny space, so I went tentatively inside.

The Master teacher appeared from around a corner. Brief conversation about my past martial arts experience and my interest now in Tai Chi. Then an amazing demonstration began. Physical feats of unbelievable balance and flexibility. But, the most fascinating of which was my being asked to push him backwards as he stood before me face to face. Without any external movement, he tightened the muscles in his body so that he was in, what he called, a "strong" position. I moved him back easily. He then asked me to put my hands on both sides of his waist. I did so. He relaxed his body completely, and I suddenly felt like my hands were around a silo, and a thousand or so pounds of grain had just dropped between my hands, with an inaudible but physically felt "whoosh!" And, I now could not budge him at all. He was just still standing in front of me, but pushing on him, with all my strength, felt like I was pushing on an extremely heavy, but soft yet unmovable pillar. It was a remarkable experience for me. Nothing had moved, but there was all that internal movement. What the hell was that? "Sinking my Chi," he said, by way of explanation. This told me absolutely nothing at the time. But I requested, then and there, to be his student. Pursuing the impossible has always intrigued me. I have spent the last 40 years exploring the mysteries and many levels of T'ai Chi Ch'uan.

The "Let's Pretend" Christmas

Somewhere in the confusion of my drop-out hippie years, I decided to drop back in, at least for awhile, and found myself temporarily back in my hometown of Minneapolis. I don't remember a lot of the specific initiating circumstances, but I was there and it was cold ... winter-in-Minnesota cold. I think that I had sublet my apartment in San Francisco to a friend, and was going to be in Minnesota for three or four months, though god knows why, and why, especially in mid winter?

The upshot of it all was that I was pretty broke, and I had perhaps thought that I might still have some helpful contacts in my home state, from my earlier, more productive and stable days. Following that line of thinking, I decided that since I had been an actor before dropping out, maybe I could act somewhere again. Why not?

Several old show-biz friends helped arrange a few auditions for me, one for the stage, and one for commercials. I was terrified. I hadn't acted onstage for a couple of years, and had done no camera acting for even longer. But somehow, god knows how, with my long, thin hair pinned up in back with artfully concealed bobby pins, I got a part in a commercial! It was to be a Christmas commercial for a well-known bank. The story idea was that a young family consisting of father, mother, and two delightful young girls, were unwrapping presents in front of their tree, and taking photos of the excitement. There would be no lines spoken (all the better), only music and a voice-over narration underneath the visuals.   The marketing angle was that the bank was giving out free cameras (just like the one in the commercial … how clever) to anyone opening a new bank account during the Christmas holidays.

Now here's the intriguing part. At that point in time, I had been divorced once, had no kids, and had not experienced a Christmas tree or gift-wrapped presents in any place that I had lived for the last five or six years. The only exception was a bit earlier in L.A. where my not-yet-ex-wife and I had bought a three foot Christmas tree nailed at the bottom to two x-shaped plywood sticks forming its base. There had been no snow, and the tree had been purchased on some barren L.A. lot that looked like a desert.   There had been little or no feeling of Christmas. Suddenly, here I was in snowy Minnesota at Christmas time, in a huge, beautiful home in a rich neighborhood, about to pretend that I was a father (in a costume of a luxurious bathrobe, pajamas and slippers) with a wife and two kids … much of which I had never experienced in my life! Some acting would definitely be required.

Well, while the crew was setting up the lights and arranging the set, and Christmas Carols were filling the house with holiday music, my commercial "wife" and I were upstairs in a gorgeous bedroom changing into our lovely costumes. Oh, yes, and a whimsical note of irony is that my commercial "wife" was actually a dear actress friend from my past. I was really nervous, but her presence relaxed me. I also had a vague feeling of melancholy from being in that very full and beautiful environment, some sense of loss, or of joys never had. But all was well as my "wife" and I chatted away pleasantly, and busily transformed ourselves into "Mom" and "Dad."

Finally, we're called to the living room set downstairs, and its stunningly decorated tree, with lights seemingly ablaze. The director suggests that I should make friends with the two little girls playing my daughters, so that we could all be comfortable, and laugh and hug each other freely during the filming. Clearly, whatever is left of the actor in me must come forth now, because I surely know little or nothing about talking with young kids, and certainly nothing at all about looking at gifts and joking about with a five-year-old "daughter" sitting on my knee. But we do talk, and laugh, and play, and it's fun. I feel warm inside.

Places please! Here we go. Action! Lots of camera shots. Lots of music. Lots of laughter. The littlest girl is especially charming, and the commercial shoot is a success. In fact, the over-all joyful quality of the piece, as well as the big eyes and radiant smile of the little girl, is such that the advertising people want to do a sequel the following week!

So, with the two commercials, I had now had a little financial success, as well as a touch of renewed self confidence. But, what I remember most, and what was the beginning of a long personal transformation, was the sense of love and joy and family and home, that I had magically experienced on such a surprisingly deep emotional level from that "let's pretend Christmas."

Resurrection

Although, early on, I had held a fairly decent job in a big-time theatre ticket office in San Francisco, had co-created a small professional theatre company there, which folded, and had even gained a teaching degree, I eventually found myself to be clearly lost and burned-out in my City by the Bay. The only reasonable answer, as I had discovered on an earlier trip to Minneapolis, seemed to be to re-sublet my San Francisco apartment and head home again to Minneapolis, where I might still have some connections, and could restart.

I borrow money to fly back. I move into a residence hotel with a small efficiency apartment, which includes a kitchenette and a Murphy bed that pulls down from the wall. Again, some small acting successes there, but nothing enduring works out. Then, a miracle! An almost desperate series of phone calls, on a borrowed office phone, to anyone who might be able to get me some work, finally pays off. The Theatre Department Chair at my former University remembers me fondly and tells me that a scheduled Guest Artist Teacher has had to cancel coming there, due to a role in a Broadway play. And would I like to take that position and teach Beginning Acting, as I had done as a graduate student a number of years before? Would I? I would!

I have only a couple of weeks to prepare. I am terrified. I am still pretty fried from my misbehaving years as an experimenting hippie, and can barely look anyone in the eye. But, I'm an actor, right? I can fake it. Which I do ... playing the part of what I imagine to be a cool, hip teacher, open to the needs and wants of his students. After the first few weeks of psyching myself up in the bathroom before each class, and returning to a stall in the john to calm down after the class, I begin to actually embrace the role and feel semi-comfortable with it. Transformation. I have become the cool-guy acting teacher. You may have heard the phrase, "Fake it 'til you make it?" Well, I did it. It was the performance of a lifetime.

I managed to keep that wonderful ego strengthening, but low-paying job for a full year. And, I parlayed that Guest-Artist position into an interview for a full-time Assistant Professor position at a University in Southern Illinois. A position which I eventually got and kept for the next 27 years, with a professional theatre career on the side. Altogether, another miracle.

IV. Openings and Closings

Wives, Ex-Wives and Other Similar Beings

In an oddly sad way, it's kind of fun to say things like "my first ex-wife, my second ex-wife, my almost-wife, my third wife" and still be able to take marriage seriously. How many times can you say something to the effect of "'til death do us part," after being apart yet still being fully alive, without breaking into a bit of an ironic smile?

Winning and Losing ... My Heart

"Don't shoot! Don't shoot!" Gleeful, boyish shouts. Then mocking laughter. It's an outdoor basketball court in a park in L.A. It's dusk. The court is lit by several strong streetlights. A small chunky boy has just somehow caught a basketball and is looking about frantically ... what to do with the ball? His fellow players, all about nine or ten years old, have plenty of advice. "Don't shoot, don't shoot," they all shout again. More laughter. My heart goes out to this child.

This same shy, awkward little boy eventually becomes my sort-of stepson. I'm in a new somewhat-relationship with his mom, an attractive actress and movement therapist, but I'm moving to the Midwest to teach. I'm still living in San Francisco, where I have re-met the mom, whom I knew years earlier, at a theatre party. She and the boy are actually living in L.A. I'm just down there now for a visit.

The next year is spent with me flying back and forth from my Midwest college town to L.A., on cheap-o midnight flights to stay with them on weekends. Several times they fly up to my place. Same overnight cheap-o flights. Even though I'm teaching full time, the salary then is minimal.

At the end of that year, exhausted from repeated late night flights, we decide that the mom and the boy should move to my town and we'll all live together. After a lot of crazed logistics, it happens. We are unmarried, it's the '70s, but we're a family.

We acquire a dog. The mom and I live and love intensely. Lots of emotional baggage from our previous lives and relationships. The boy's father had passed away soon after the boy was born. I teach the boy to play baseball. Some smiling memories of my own dad. All is going relatively well. At one point, I even find myself telling the boy that I know all of his friends have real dads, and if it would be easier for him to call me Dad when he is with them, that would be cool with me. I think he looked down and quietly managed an "ok" and a trace of a smile.

Four years go by. Somewhere in there, on a vacation back to California, in which we leave the dog behind in the care of friends, an early morning call informs us that our little dog has been hit by a car and has died. Trauma all around! Lots of quick changing of plans. The mom and boy fly home early. For some reason, I have to stay in the Bay Area for a few more days. The next day, I get another early morning call. The mom tearfully informs me that not only have we lost our sweet dog, but the dog has left a legacy ... our apartment has become totally infested with fleas! She tells me that she and the boy are leaving our place to stay with friends for a few days while the apartment is professionally flea-bombed. Very sad, but strangely funny too.

Our family life continues for awhile, but the intense emotions of the relationship between the mom and I finally drive us apart. I miss both of them … but my heart is left with the boy.

A Kind of Zen Whack

Imagine spending 11 out of 18 months in three separate trips to Hawaii ... partially subsidized at that! Not a bad deal. Somehow I pulled off these trips as sabbaticals, developmental leaves, and summer research grants from my University in the mid 1980s. Those kinds of leaves of absence, sorry to say, are seldom to be found in academia anymore!

Well, after all my years of tai chi study and teaching it, I was definitely intrigued by PR China. So, I finally managed to get a research grant to study Asian Theatre at the University of Hawaii. Suffice it to say that much academic knowledge was gained, but even more awareness occurred on the personal level, especially concerning intercultural awarenesses.

At one point, in the second trip I believe, the Theatre faculty at the University of Hawaii brought to the Honolulu Campus, The National Kabuki Theatre of Japan, direct from Tokyo. An enormously large company of highly talented traditional, stylized theatre actors. The company was to offer some workshops for students as well as a week's worth of public performances. I was able to participate in all of it, including observation of the dressing rooms, as the actors worked with all the elaborate costumes and makeup. Amazing!

At one midway point in the week, the faculty arranged for the group of male actors who portrayed the female Onnagata characters to be taken out to dinner as a group (there were, at the time, no women performers in traditional Kabuki theatre). For some long forgotten reason, none of the faculty was available that evening to escort them. As a professor myself, I was politely asked by a faculty member if I would do the honor of escorting and dining with these fine performers. Yes, of course, I said. The only unforeseen dilemma by me was that none of the actors spoke English, at least as I thought then, not well. I guess we were taken in cars or a van to the restaurant, so that was easy enough, as was finding our reserved long table. I sat in the middle, with a young actor opposite me. The food was served, and everyone commenced chatting fairly loudly, except it was all in Japanese! All I really remember was that I somehow managed to discover that the young actor opposite me knew a few words of English. We exchanged minimal basic words and phrases and a few mime-like gestures to enable a kind of minimalist dialogue between us. This continued throughout the evening, while all the Japanese chatting continued on around us. Finally, the evening drew to an end, and we were somehow returned to the actors' hotel, and I returned to where I was living. While being a bit nerve wracking, it had been a quite pleasant evening.

The Big Zen whack occurred the next afternoon, when the professor who had arranged all this, saw me in the hall and asked how the evening had gone. I recall saying that it was quite enjoyable, but that none of them could speak English, which made it a bit difficult. She asked if that meant I didn't talk to anyone for the entire evening. "Oh, no," I said, "I was able to talk a little to the young actor opposite me." She seemed to both frown and smile slightly as she said, "So you mean to say that you speak no Japanese, and that 'no one could speak any English,' but that a conversation was somehow sustained between you and that young actor throughout an entire two hour dinner? I would say that that young actor knew a lot of English." I'm sure that I stammered and turned red with embarrassment, as my "ugly American" shortsightedness hit home. I have never forgotten that lesson. Having personally struggled culturally and linguistically now through two subsequent, lengthy trips to China, I try to help people from other countries with language communication difficulties here in the USA wherever and whenever I can.

Mystery Man Revisited

My dad could not ever stop drinking for long. Over all the years, I could never understand that. He often went regularly to AA for awhile ... and he was smart. But he'd start drinking again. Why couldn't he finally quit, and stay quit?

Then one year, when I was visiting Minneapolis near the end of one of his month long drinking "binges," as he called them, I found out. Dad and I had a screaming argument in his messy studio apartment, in which he finally stunned me into silence. He shouted that in the Army he had been under heavy air bombardment in the railroad yards overseas for 53 nights in a row, and "What the Hell did I know about anything anyway?"

What? Wow ... silence ... I think I mumbled some form of, "I'm so sorry ... I didn't know I had no idea...." More silence.

After a time, my dad began to talk. He shared his feelings from that War of so long ago. "What do you think it was like," he said, "to be sitting ducks in a shack in an open train yard, playing cards and drinking straight booze, night after night, with enemy bombs dropping all around you, knowing that you had a newborn, furlough-baby son back in the States that you have never seen, and knowing that you could be blown to pieces at any second?" I had nothing more to say. Nothing more I could say ... then. I hugged him, I think, and I left.

Later, alone in a bar somewhere, I realized that I could not even begin to conceive of what my dad must have gone through in his three years in that war—being stationed in three different countries, on two different continents, having to learn parts of three different languages, missing his wife and and his son, and always the terrifying, nightly bombings screaming overhead— because, wherever he was, the railroad yards were the supply lines and were always the target. Not that those bombings, and every unimaginable else that he must have undergone during wartime, was a full justification for his forty-plus years of basically nonstop drinking, but those 53 consecutive nights of bombing sure made a dent in my self-righteous, misguided judgment about him.

I wish that we had had that talk earlier in our lives, and that we had been able to share so much more ... the mystery man.

Flying with Dad

I'm flying! At least I feel like I'm flying. I'm running back, chasing and catching a long fly ball over my shoulder, off the bat of my dad. It feels great!

Now, years later, I'm flying to Minneapolis in a snow storm in February to see my dad in the Veterans' Hospital before he dies. He's been comatose for three days, having had a ruptured tumor in his stomach, which has poisoned his entire body. Keeping him alive has meant continuous flushing of his system with fluids so that he looks like a swollen, giant-headed monster ... unrecognizable. His body is so toxic that I am told not to touch him without putting on surgical gloves. I refuse and hold his hand.

I guess that he cannot hear me, but he might be in there somewhere, so I tell him about his hitting those long fly balls to me, and how glad and grateful I am that he taught me how to play ball. Motionless, and with his eyes closed in that massive head, a tear somehow emerges from his right eye and rolls ever so slowly down his right cheek. My sister, who has been there for three days, comes in and says that it's almost the end of lunchtime in the commissary. I see his vital-signs monitor blinking and am reluctant to leave, but we are reassured by a nurse, and we go.

When we return, a tall, nicely dressed woman is standing outside Dad's door. I know immediately that he has died. With a gentle smile, she tells us it's true, and escorts us into the room. In death, he's even more unrecognizable. He's lying on his side now, in some kind of semi-contorted position. I touch his hand again. This kind woman, who has been Dad's social worker, talks to us over his twisted body. She makes us smile with her pleasant reminiscences of what a funny and charming character my dad has been over the years. About twenty minutes later, she has talked us down to a peaceful state, stopping our tears. It's time to leave. I touch his hand again. I fly home.

New Wife, Las Vegas, No Elvis

It's 1991. I've just come back from a second trip to China. A number of years and a number of relationships have gone by. That old '60s and '70s hippie attitude of free-flowing relationships has not been fully rescinded in my mind.

A very pretty young woman, whom I have met before, materializes in one of my classes. A gradual attraction and mutual intrigue occurs, and we begin to date a bit. As youthful as she seems at age twenty-six, she is considered a nontraditional student. According to the unwritten academic rules of the time, she is fully an adult and can make her own rules. Romance is possible between us.

However, a general rule of relationship stability has something to do with both parties being of similar ages, which was another matter entirely. This young woman and I were twenty-two years apart when we first got together. The years between us did not magically lessen as the years went by. In fact, it seemed as if the age difference increased. As a youthful, fun-loving forty-eight-year-old at the outset, I had no problem relating to and keeping up with my young soon-to-be wife. We had a delightful and surprisingly sweet Las Vegas wedding. Instead of the optional "Elvis" minister, we had a gentle and wise missionary minister on leave from his tropical saving of souls. However, as the years continued to roll by, an increasing number of divergent interests and paths began to grow. Going out to sing at Karaoke bars in the wee hours, amid boisterous young businessmen drunks, for example, was not a good fit for me, nor were many other social events, her job changes, and business travels. I was beginning to have more affection for home and hearth. My dear wife was a smart, multi-talented and kind person, but our ten-year marriage finally dissolved. Besides, I can't sing anyway.

Challenges

A phone call comes in. Mom has had a moderate stroke.
Several weeks later she has another one. It's much worse.
My sister and I both live in different cities. Working
together by phone with varying medical and legal
authorities is not easy. We finally find a nursing home
that can and will take Mom in.

My mother never swore. Ever. Well, maybe a "damn,"
once or twice in my lifetime.

Until, that first nursing home. As a huge male orderly
was trying awkwardly to lift Mom to put her into bed, I
appeared in the doorway just in time to hear her yell out,
"Goddamn you!"

What? My ever-religious mom can't even talk since this
frustrating stroke, except for partial phrases or partial
songs sometimes ... but this? I was shocked, but I smiled,
and helped put her to bed.

The clumsy orderly was not the only torture my
mother encountered there. On another visit, a month or
so later, I was searching for Mom, who was not in her
room, and finally found her in the physical therapy room.
I was just about to enter when I heard her shout out in
pain. Mom was seated in her wheelchair and the two PT
people were trying to extend and lift one of her legs to a

straight out position. Mom shouted out again. I rushed in saying, "What the hell are you doing to her?"

"Well, they said, we've got to get her range of motion back." "She's 86 years old, and in a wheelchair," I yell. "If her range of motion for her leg is only three inches upward, that's enough, dammit! Causing her pain while stretching her leg for an unreachable goal is bullshit!" I wheeled my mom out of the room.

My sister and I had my mom moved to another nursing home. It was lovely. It was run by a religious organization, and the people who worked there were very attentive and kind. Finally, Mom was settled into a place of pleasantness and peace. She had quite a few visitors there, and was generally content. Yet, she often tried to escape to the sunlight and the squirrels outside by cleverly learning how to operate the push-button door from her wheelchair and sneaking outside. The staff said that they had found her, several times, out in the park which bordered the nursing home. That made me smile. Mom was always an independent spirit.

Missing Things

The Peoples' Republic of China is a long way from NordEast Minneapolis. I'm somewhere in the midst of my four-month trip to China. I've extended my three week University sponsored tour in order to do personal research on Traditional Chinese Theatre, and to further explore this strange and fascinating "foreign" land. It's 1990, the summer after the infamous "Tiananmen Square Massacre." Every day, when my morning studies are over, I am totally on my own. Speaking barely 200 words of Mandarin, with a tattered Chinese phrase book as a constant bible-like companion, it's all a bit daunting, to say the least.

Missing things is a major factor. Having eaten only Chinese food, as tasty as it is, for all three meals a day for several months now, I find myself hungry for familiar foods. This extends to a hunger for familiar faces, which extends to just missing the sounds of the English language.

To the rescue. AT&T, the CIA, and Campbell's soup!

On a beautiful but lonely Sunday afternoon, I'm craving new tastes and old friends. I make my way to a grand international hotel which is said to have extensive buffets of American food each Sunday. They do. It's fantastic! From eggs Benedict to cream puffs, it's every taste treat I could imagine. Fully stuffed and smiling, I waddle outside, and decide to brave the unimaginably overcrowded bus lines to place a call to the States. I call three friends.

Only their answering machines respond. I'm depressed. As I try a fourth call, the pleasant female AT&T operator detects the apparent groans in my voice, and asks me, if anything is wrong. I babble something about being alone in China, and not reaching several friends just now. She says, in her delightfully perky voice, that she'll talk to me. What? How wonderful! She does. We chat. We laugh. I think I must be in an AT&T commercial. She says she has to go. I thank her, from deep places within me. I hang up, and head back to the ordeal of the buses, but with a bit of a bounce in my step and a smile again on my face.

On another seeking-someone-to-talk-with-in-English occasion, I meet a guy in a bar near the U.S. Embassy who suggests that he is with the CIA. He tells me of another bar, called "Frank's Place," which is Chinese owned, but which serves lots of Embassy folks and also serves authentic American Cheeseburgers, with real mustard or ketchup. This bar proves to be a major discovery! The same fellow also tells me about a seemingly miraculous 7-Eleven type store to be found in the basement of another major western hotel on the outskirts of Beijing.

Again on a Sunday, again braving the crowded buses, I head out on a very long ride toward the airport, seeking the suggested 7-Eleven. I find it. It's an oasis! As I wander its narrow aisles, discovering boxes and cans of American comfort foods, like macaroni and cheese, I am filled with a mysterious contentment. Seeing the rows of brightly colored cans of Campbell's soup, my eyes tear up. I feel like I'm home. But I wonder what life must be like for a true immigrant who has left behind the foods, friends, family, and customs of his own country forever?

Talking with Mom

Not the best choice. But all things considered, no real regrets. Why I made that choice, however, I have no idea anymore.

It was Spring break from my job at the University. I was going to visit both my mom, in her nursing home in Minneapolis, and a dear Chinese friend and his family then living in D.C./Virginia. Where to go first? For some reason, I chose to see my friend first. Someone's schedule? Cheaper flying routes? More logical flight connections on the return? Who knows now.

So, I've flown to D.C. I'm staying with my friend and his family for three days. On the second day I'm sightseeing in downtown D.C. when my cell phone rings. It's my sister, who's calling from Minneapolis. "Mom is definitely getting more frail." That is what she says. What I hear in my brain is, "Mom is probably dying soon." My sister is there at the nursing home with her youngest son, a cool, kind, 20-something young man, and they are taking care of Mom, and are often sitting with her. "I'm flying in tomorrow afternoon," I say, "but should I try to get an even earlier flight?" "No," my sister says. "There's nothing you could do … hopefully Mom will still be OK when you get here." I'm still hearing, "dying soon." A flood of feelings ... sightseeing suddenly seems meaningless. I wander about vacantly for a time and then head back to my friend's place.

That night I go up to the guest room about 10 p.m. I try to read for a bit. But I'm scattered. Eventually, I sleep. In a few hours I wake up to go to the bathroom. When I return to bed, I'm restless. For some reason I had brought along a photo of my mom and myself. I pull it out and gaze at it for a long time. Lots of thoughts ... lots of feelings ... I close my eyes. "Mom," I finally say to her, "if you are really tired and just want to let go now, it's ok. You don't have to wait for me." I mull this over, and realize that I mean it, even if it means not seeing her alive again. I repeat this several times, "If you want to let go now, it's ok." Eyes closed, I am at peace, and drift off.

Two hours later, about 2 a.m., the family phone downstairs begins to ring. Incessantly. I'm in a fog. No one stirs to answer it. A sudden premonition. I rush bumblingly downstairs in the dark. No idea where any light switches are. I grab and almost drop the miraculously discovered still ringing phone. It's my sister. "Mom has just died," she says. "We've been here holding her hand. It's ok. She was peaceful." I am stunned, but find myself thinking, with some wonder, how Mom and I seem to have connected, even without my being there.

The Last Little Dog

The door bell rang in the morning, and my second ex-wife, who was still my wife at the time, was coming back from her morning walk...with a gorgeous fluffy all-white puppy dog cradled in her arms.

How often does a Chinese Crested Powder Puff puppy show up on your doorstep?

As much as I enjoy playing with little dogs or big dogs, I am far too selfish to want to have one. My personal freedom to do what I want, whenever I want, as best I can, precludes the desire to have to walk the dog, on a daily or twice daily basis. Besides, eventually, or way too soon, they always die on you.

When I was nine or ten years old, I had my first pet (other than a turtle ... who of course also died) and he was a small combination mutt dog, of terrier and Labrador extraction. I named him Tippy because he had a little white tip on his tail, as well as a little patch of white at his throat, peeking forth from his otherwise all smooth and shiny black body. I know I loved that dog, but nearly all I can really remember about him is that after several years he developed what the then vet called leukemia. As Tippy began to lose control of his legs, it was determined in our family somehow, that since we did not have a car, and

Tippy was, after all, "my" pet, that I was the one who should responsibly drive him in my bike's handlebar basket to the vet's office to have him put to sleep. This sad, sad, scary task I did, in an early evening rather than daylight, for some long forgotten reason. I think I vowed then not to have another pet ... ever ... 'cuz it was all too sad.

I never did have another dog until 20 some years later, by which time I had somehow also acquired a relationship that came with a semi-grown kid. This small boy was about the same age as I had been when I acquired Tippy. Of course this young boy also wanted a dog. Since he and his mother had just recently moved in with me, from across the country, I tried my selfish best to be accommodating, and we all got a new dog. He was a small Scottish terrier, appropriately named Scottie by the boy. I enjoyed this playful, funny looking little dog. Of course the dog had to be walked, which I also did for my fair share of the time. Unfortunately, Scottie met with a most un-expected demise. While our family was away on a trip to CA., the people who had volunteered to care for Scottie, phoned us to say he had been hit and killed by a car. More great sadness all around. The fact that Scottie had mysteriously left a legacy of a plethora of fleas in our apartment during our absence, only added to the pain.

Memories. No more dogs, I vowed again.

Back to the almost then present. The Chinese Crested Powder Puff. This stunningly beautiful, nearly show-level little dog, came in the door with my then wife, and almost immediately won my heart. Over several days, we tracked down the owners of the lost puppy. They didn't want her back because she kept running away. But, she was a pure-bread, and we had to pay them for her. We did. She already had seemed to belong with us.

My wife worked full time, and I was teaching with a less regulated schedule, so I got to walk the dog most often, even twice daily. I somehow learned to almost enjoy those ritual, but essential, walks in our nearby park. At home the little dog and I played on the floor together a lot. We playfully roughhoused. We hugged. Her name had become Penny. She was sweet.

Of course, as we know, nothing much besides oceans and mountains often lasts. That marriage didn't either. Penny, who had been found by my wife, went with my wife. Another little dog gone. The last dog.

The Big Question

"**H**ow do you deal with all that loss?" "Huh?" Wasn't ready for that. It's the question my younger sister blurts out, when pressed by me asking, "Isn't there anything that you want to know about me?" We're sitting in my living room, both in our early sixties.

Quickly and glibly I say something fairly trite about people simply growing apart from each other over time in a relationship. That "it's perfectly normal. You love. You come together for a time, you both learn and grow from it. You change, and sometimes you just move on." Sounded good at the time, and was the first thing that popped out of my mouth, after having to instantaneously question my entire existence in relationships. My sister nods skeptically but semi-acceptingly. Our lengthy conversation about who we were in our lives while mostly distanced from each other, both geographically and emotionally, moves onward.

But, it's a helluva good question.

The Best For Last, At Last

Having similar interests and similar backgrounds is often a good omen for a successful relationship. Try, for example, a man and a woman, from modest economic backgrounds, but who are both college educated, and have parallel interests and actual experience in martial arts, acting, life-coaching, and new-age "spirituality." Such unusual parallels! Candidates for a "marriage made in Heaven?" Not so fast.

Other variables do factor in. Such as, introvert/extrovert, neat/cluttered, spontaneous/cautious, and every other polar opposite known to man or woman as a source of potential personality and relationship conflict. And yet. There is love. That inexplicable mystery which can, despite all rational odds, bond two people together in enduring romance and partnership.

I now have my forever-wife—Sunshine Rainbow Warrior Queen, as I like to think of her, for her many positive personal energies and the positive effects she has on me. Whatever differences and difficulties we encounter, it seems that either one or the other of us has enough common sense and maturity to help the other poor fool see the error of their ways. Or not. Sometimes we just argue until something gets miraculously resolved.

But, we don't just throw in the towel and move on. That's a big step for me.

We've been together now, in some form of relationship for fourteen years. For the first three years, since we were both gun-shy-as-hell from each being recently divorced, we called it a "non-relationship." Our friends laughed. For the last seven years, we lived together, and exactly three years ago in March, on the first day of spring, we got married. Now that's a bit of a tale.

How to finally propose, I wondered. Especially since it would be for the third time ... as well as for it having taken so very long to occur. It needed to be something special ... something theatrical perhaps, but something deeply from the heart. What to do? Hmmm....

Finally, an idea. Our favorite restaurant. Our favorite table. A place where we've had many a romantic glass of wine or a meal ... and a place where we are well-known by the staff. The plan, a faux Special Delivery package, with a beautiful card, a hand-printed proposal, and a special necklace inside. The dilemma, how to make it happen?

Suddenly, it's just two days before the intended, momentous deed. Much has to occur: A number of urgent phone calls to try to reach a favorite waitress to enlist her aid in the romantic plot. Two hurried visits to the local post office to buy an official, large post office envelope, as well as to pilfer as many flashy looking stickers of a "Special Delivery, Certified Mail, or Return Signature Requested," nature as possible. The more stickers the better! Searching for and finding "the" most romantic card ever written, and adding my personal loving proposal to it. Stuffing the envelope with the card, my hand-printed proposal, along with a lovely topaz necklace to match her earlier topaz commitment ring which she is already wearing. Finally, adding hastily secured bubble-wrap with which to camouflage the flatness of the card and necklace, and to create a mysterious looking Special Delivery "package" ... all the while making numerous frustrating errors with much of this frenzied madness!

Two days later, the day of reckoning. Nerves. My about-to-be fiancée would be coming home soon from her often harried workday, expecting to go out for a relaxing, happy hour drink at our favorite place. Oh, oh! I suddenly realize that I had not considered the need to conceal the package from her, while keeping it in my possession both during the drive, as well as entering the restaurant. An absurd idea occurs! I scramble frantically for duct tape, with which to tape the package to the inside of my cool leather sport coat, on my left side, away from any straying passenger eyes.

We arrive at the restaurant, package unseen. So far, so good. But how to smuggle the package, secured within my sport coat, to the conspiring waitress...and will she even be there on time? Sweaty palms. As we enter I spot the waitress behind the bar, and with sudden inspiration, tell my almost-fiancée that I have to run to the men's room, and to please order me a wine. As I dash off, I am still racking my brain for a plan to get to the waitress behind the bar, with my package, without being seen by my beloved.

Plotting furiously in the bathroom, while unthinkingly ripping my soft coat lining as I frantically try to tear off the duct tape and remove the uncooperative package from its hiding place, I am startled by the sudden intrusion of a bus boy who utters, "I hear you've got something for me." "Huh? Oh! Yes, give me a second." He leaves. Finishing the extraction of the hostile package from my garment, I realize that I have been left with no idea at all of where this possible savior will be when I emerge from this anxiety chamber.

Still panicky, I ease open the bathroom door, and there to my relief, he is! In the shadows of the wall, his back toward me, he is cagily holding his arm behind his back, palm up, awaiting my entrance, and deliverance of the precious envelope. He takes it, and surreptitiously saunters behind the bar to deliver the goods to the complicit waitress. Whew. I regain some composure, and head back to our table. I smile and calmly greet my dear one, by now sipping her wine, with a glass waiting welcomingly for me.

All the rest of the plan goes amazingly well. At a pre-arranged signal, the waitress taps my fiancée-to-be on the shoulder, saying, "Excuse me, but a package was just delivered at the back door, and the address on it says it's for you. This is you, isn't it?" A great look of incredulity fills my partner's lovely face. "Well, yes," she says, taking the stickered-up, official looking package addressed to her. Her eyes dart inquiringly to me, with a goofy smile creeping onto her face.

Suffice it to say, the package is opened. The necklace is admired. The perfect card and proposal are read. Some tears emerge around the edges of her eyes, and an answer of "yes" is smilingly whispered to me.

Time goes by. We are finally married in a civil ceremony at the courthouse by a judge friend of ours, on the very first day of spring. It's a beautiful day.

V. KEEPING THINGS INTERESTING

Crazy Man

I'm trotting along on a dirt road of an imagined Civil War town, pleading with an imaginary figure who is riding beside me on an imaginary horse. The setting is a major Hollywood film, being shot in a small, formerly flooded-out town in Missouri which has been transformed into a war-ravaged film set. No actual filming is occurring. I've arrived early for my week of shooting, and everyone is at lunch ... no one's around. So, as the conscientious actor-creature that I am, I've found my way to the set and am rehearsing my lines while running, shouting, and gesticulating up toward the imaginary rider. I'm working on the timing of my lines with the distance I imagine that I would have to run to finish the speech. "An actor prepares." I'm being prepared ... or so I thought.

Eventually, cast members and production crews begin returning from lunch. I, of course, stop running and shouting in the road. I am escorted to my costume fittings, given a tentative shooting schedule for my scenes, and told I am free to watch the shots scheduled for the day. I am happy to do that. While I have been a member of the actors' unions since my mid-20s, I've primarily been a stage director and acting teacher for the past 20 years or so. To suddenly find myself acting in a major feature film is not without a high degree of nervous anticipation!

My first day of actual shooting is, in fact, that same running-down-the-street scene shouting up at the rider on horseback. It does not go at all as I had imagined (practical film acting lesson #1)!

First of all, there is a real flesh-and-blood rider, who looks like a young Buffalo Bill. Secondly, he has been directed to ride his big horse down the boardwalk of the town, not the actual road I had imagined, and I am to jog along beside him between the horse and the very tightly spaced wooden hitching rails, and also to jump up and down a step or two at both the end of the "block" and the beginning of the next one. This is not an easy task. The horse is huge. I could get squashed. Keeping my eyes up on the rider while saying my lines makes negotiating the steps, without stumbling, a very tricky thing to do. Also, I am told by the the director, via an assistant director, to keep looking about somewhat wildly, as 200 horse riders are charging down the road and burning and looting the town. I do not do well. I'm apparently even shouting too loud, as the mics make up the difference needed for volume. The director calls for a number of takes. We finally finish. It seems ok, but I feel that I've gotten off to a shaky start, for someone who is a professional actor. There's lots I clearly don't know about filming.

Many exciting and interesting events occur during the week of shooting, including having my shirts wired for explosive charges for when I am to be shot and killed by that same, now bad-guy, horse-back rider in a later scene. I eat popcorn and watch an LA Lakers basketball game on TV in the lobby of the cast's motel with one the stars of the film. I get lessons in the Polish dialect that my character uses, and am told by the dialect coach that I've done well in my preparation. I get falling and dying tips via twenty minutes of rehearsal time from a veteran stunt choreographer. I even get some laughs and applause from the crew after a take on one of my scenes. So things are going better since that first day. And finally, comes the big day ... my death scene.

OK. It turns out that the bad-guy rider-on-the-horse character doesn't like my little Polish guy character very much at all. After the raider guys, who have looted and burnt the town, are beginning to gallop away, I wave and say good-bye to the horse guy (we've shared a drink in my little office, as I try to suck-up to him to save my life), and he turns suddenly, while on his horse next to me, and shoots me point blank in the chest, killing me instantly!

Now that's what is supposed to happen. What actually happens is that at the sound of the gunshot his horse rears up, pushing the rider's face and his gun out of the camera's frame. This is bad. We do about five takes. The horse rears up every time. This is not good. On each take my shirt explodes with blood, and I have to be immediately fitted right there on the set for a new exploding shirt. Finally, the costumer says to the first assistant director, "This is the last matching shirt like that we've got. You have to get the shot right this time." Who ever thought about needing five or six exploding shirts for a death scene? Director and assistant directors huddle. A decision is made. We've already got a wider, establishing shot of the shooter guy on his horse. We'll put the shooter guy on a ladder, they say. "Just like in the movies," I think. The close-up of his face and the gun will be stable. Someone brings and adjusts a tall step ladder, with the rider straddling the top of it. I am successfully killed. No more exploding shirts are required. All is well ... just as the sun begins to go down.

One final thing. Remember my first day, running up and down that deserted main road of the town, shouting out to the imaginary rider on the imaginary horse, thinking I was alone? Well, after the final shot of my death scene, with the costumers and production staff still hovering around me, chatting and tidying up, some of the extras hired to be townspeople start emerging from the background and begin tentatively to approach me. They're not actors at all, but real townspeople from the area, hired to be extras. Finally a group of them more or less surrounds me, and they begin asking for my autograph. I'm surprised. I had only had three or four short scenes in the film over a week's time, but I'm happy to oblige. Then I hear it. "'Cuz you'se a movie star! We was eating inside a building on the set, and when we seen you running and yelling up and down the street, shouting at nobody over and over, we thought you'se a crazy man. You're a movie star, but we thought you'se a crazy man."

The Best Curtain Call Ever

I had been a dues paying, card-carrying member of all three professional acting unions since I was 26 years old. And I was very proud of that. But, by the time I was 68, I hadn't acted in a stage play for 25 years! I kept paying all my semi-annual dues because membership in the professional acting unions made my resume for teaching and conducting acting workshops look good. God knows how much money I had spent over all the years on union dues ... but at least they were tax deductible.

One day, in my 68th year, a friend and well respected stage director asked me to be in a play. "A small part in an ensemble piece," he said. After much internal debate, and some encouraging discussions with my wife, I agreed to do it. I'd be a paid professional actor again. Wow, how fun! Instead, it turned out to be a big part, lots of difficult poetic lines to learn, and by opening night I was terrified. What if I forget my lines? I was "old"—it was hard to remember them. But it was a very creative project and came off quite well.

So, over the next three years, I was asked to do another one. And then another one. That third one, for a different theatre, was the one with the fun curtain call.

I was playing a crotchety old man, something I had

often done many times earlier in my career when I was young and not yet a crotchety old man. I was a character actor, and could transform my voice and body and mind quite believably into an old guy. Here I was, 40 years later, playing an old guy who, according to the script, was probably younger than I now actually was, as a for real old guy.

I rehearsed my lines a lot … way before rehearsals started. I did it in my living room, and on my walks in the neighborhood parks, and around the track at the gym. I would mumble my lines aloud, in a scratchy Cockney accent, and my body would fall into the more stooped shape and gait of this old character. People around me looked, and then looked away. Was this old coot crazy or what? Talking to himself in broad daylight, not even a visible cell phone to justify it.

Well, eventually, it was opening night. We had finally arranged the order and spacing for the curtain call just before the audience was to be let into the theatre. The play went well, getting both lots of laughs and being pretty shocking at times emotionally. Suddenly, we were in the final scene. I was offstage, trapped in an unseen area where I had supposedly gone to die, having been kicked to almost death on stage some 20 minutes earlier. It occurred to me at this very moment before the curtain call, that the director had never said whether we should come out, still physically as our characters, or to just run out as ourselves and bow. Curtain calls are sometimes done either way. I only had a few seconds to decide. Suddenly, it came to me in a flash. I figured that since I had suffered so much to play this role, walking all stooped over and developing an aching back, rehearsing for so many months in advance, getting beaten up on stage, and then having to hide backstage in an uncomfortable area, making no sound, for 20 minutes every night, that I deserved a little extra glory.

So, as the lights came up, and I was to take my bow, I walked out in my character walk, with my funny looking old-man glasses, for about three or four steps, so the audience could perceive me as they had seen me. But then, I suddenly whipped off my goofy glasses, stood up straight, broke into a youthful run to my position, and bowed with a bit of a flourish. To my delight, the audience let out a collective gasp, then laughed, as they fully realized and appreciated the difference between the old character they had believed that they were watching in the play, and the far more youthfully spry person that I as the actor actually was. I loved it!

The director later smilingly said, "Well that was a pretty interesting curtain call, but go ahead and keep doing it." I did. It always gave me a rush, and made the whole difficult role worthwhile. The best curtain call ever!

Being Bent Over

My wife and I are having a glass of wine in the bar area of one of our favorite restaurants where my special delivery proposal had occurred. I excuse myself and head off to the bathroom, a not uncommon occurrence when imbibing alcohol in one's early seventies. I'm about 10-12 feet away when my wife calls out after me, in a semi-loud whisper, "stand up straight." I realize immediately that I must be slumped over again. I've been walking like an "old man," even older than I am, for the past several weeks. I had just recently finished playing the "crotchety old guy" in the play with the "Best Curtain Call Ever."

While it may seem that conveying an old man by walking bent over, with somewhat slow, shuffling steps, would be clichéd acting, all you have to do is observe elderly people at a market or mall to understand that clichés are rooted in truth, and are even suggested by the scripts. It fits audience expectations. But you do have to do it truthfully. The problem, after forcing your body to bend over like that, after several months of rehearsing and performing, is being able to let go of those physical changes which have, over time, programmed themselves into the body with a kind of muscle memory.

Beyond this instance in the bar, an even more strange "bent-over" occurrence happened earlier at home, in the very room that I had rehearsed that particular old man character daily for nearly three months. One week after the show closed, I got up from the living room sofa, to head upstairs. Then it happened! As I began to pass through the very hallway and living room where I had rehearsed that bent-over character, oh so many times, my body suddenly dropped into a semi version of that actual old man's body! I had taken three or four steps before I realized what was happening. I was stunned. Then I smiled as I straightened up. Another magical experience!

The Amazing Roto-Rooter Tool ... for People

What could it possibly look like? How can it do all that it does? In such a small space! I suppose I could look it up, Google it, but that wouldn't be as much fun as trying to imagine it. It can apparently nip, snip, sew, tuck, tie, and probably much more, all while I remain unaware of anything at all even happening. "'Cuz I am out. Like a light." It's a colonoscopy!

The second one in less that a year! All because the first one missed a section of my colon. The colonoscopy could not be completed because somehow a part of my colon was not completely cleansed before the procedure. This, despite my dutiful attempts to follow all the purification rituals required. All that fasting, all that distasteful and unpleasant laxative torture! Now it's almost time to grin and bare it again. My anxiety mounts. Just one day before the fasting and full-gallon-of-laxative chugging begins. And then there will be the bathroom ... and again ... and again ... and again. There will be little sleep. When the actual day of reckoning arrives, at about 6 a.m., I will be driven to the hospital ... totally groggy, starving, and with a very chafed bum. On the drive, I will do my best to fantasize that the expected nipping, snipping, sewing, tucking, and tying is already over. Nothing bad will be found. I will be escorted to the car in a pleasantly stoned recovery haze. My sweet, beautiful wife will drive me home, where I will sleep and dream of filets and pasta and wine, with a gentle smile on my finally peaceful face.

PART TWO:

Musings and Mutterings of a Playfully Crotchety Old Man

(Griv-isms)

I. KEEPING IT LIGHT

Simple and Silly

Keep it Simple
　　Make It Better

　　　　　　　　　　　Just Do Some Good
　　　　　　　　　　　And Have Some Fun

'Cuz, It's All Pretty Silly
　　Really
　　　　　Anyway
　　　　　　　　Isn't it?

Sox

The comfy, cushy enemy … reminding me repeatedly

That I can no longer bend over easily.

Belts

The Teaching Assistant to "Sox,"

Bending over is waaaay more fun when not wearing
belts …

Sighing with relief, without groaning in pain.

Short-Lived Inspiration

The man who couldn't do anything
Thought he wanted to,
Tried a few,
Decided he didn't.

New Year's Eve, Getting Older

I'm psyching myself up

   To go to a late night party

Where the oldest person there

   Will be younger

Than I can ever remember being

Considerations

You know, I'd rather be mellow and Happy
But being fucked-up Drunk
Ain't bad either.

Wives

Having even a semi-traditional wife is Great!
It can be a bit like having a very caring and devoted
servant …

Except she's the Boss.

Where's the Fun?

As you climb a mountain, or struggle through a
jungle, one does have to, as they say, "redefine your
definition of Fun." As we age, that becomes even
more true, and more difficult. All that used to be fun is
"not good for you" now, or you no longer can even do
it!

Things That Used to Matter to Ya
And Then They Don't

Your favorite books
Your favorite records
Your favorite video tapes
Travel to exotic places
Spicy foods
Weekends
Parties
Regular sex

Hmmm....

Even some friends...?

Not enough Time.

A Reflection on Youth

They've never been married

Never been divorced

Nobody ever died on 'em

They don't know shit

Changing Views

As the days roll by,
It takes less and less activity
to comprise a day of meaningful accomplishments.

"Back in the day," there were more activities than
could be counted.

Now, going to the store and washing some clothes
feels like a full day in itself.

Soon, getting the mail, and making the bed will be
overwhelming tasks.

II. YIKES, OTHER PEOPLE

Space

You cannot make genuine space in your heart for a
woman
While you simultaneously are finding yourself
reluctant
To make genuine space for her in your
house.

Choose People

Choose People

  Because When All is Said and Done

     A Book Can't

Hold your Hand

Lucky

I am what I am. I've done what I've done.
Without me doing much of anything more, new people
appear and previous people reappear in
my life. Interesting things continue to happen.

I'm a lucky man! Who I ultimately will have been
or will be, remains to be seen.

An OK Companion

Someone to talk "at" and "to," at least,
even if not "with."

The Reciprocal Circle

The simple version of a healthy, loving relationship is
when each partner does his or her best

To make Life

   Easier

     Happier

       And More Stimulating

For each other ... as well as for themselves

Marriage?

There are only three reasons for a man to marry, other than maybe wanting kids:

Sex.
Someone to go to the movies with.
Someone to share the difficulties of life with.

And, if you either hurt her feelings, or piss her off, you don't get any of those three things

So, it's "Yes Dear, Yes Dear, Yes Dear."

Helping

Trying to Help ...
No greater Gift to Give,
No Gift more easily Misunderstood.

Caring

When reaching out to people with difficulties,
you can't always help them, but you will, at least,
be letting them know that someone cares....

Have a Heart

He or she has a really good heart. She or He just
doesn't know how to use it yet.

III. Some Theatre Thoughts

OK

In my impassioned youth
I often said, "OK Sucks!"

In today's difficult world
To be OK enough, is OK …

Unless it's Theatre that is only OK
Then, "OK" still sucks!

Acting and Plumbing

Being an actor is like being a plumber. You have to have some actual skills. Talent and intuitive gifts are not enough to be a professional artist. If you hire a plumber to fix a clogged up toilet, and he stood around looking inept, waiting for inspiration, you would fire his ass, and look for another plumber.

Acting Shakespeare

Find out what you mean … and mean it!

The Greatest Art Form

Live Theatre is the greatest art form in the history of the world, and has been around for 2,500 years! It utilizes every other art form — from Dance to Music to Design to Puppetry, even to Media, and every other Art form in between. Name even one Art form that has not been used in Theatre. Think about it.

And, IF, only one actor gives a shoddy or just OK performance, turning the audience off, or boring them, to the point where they say, "See, I knew we should have gone to the movies," then that actor will have personally contributed to the destruction of 2,500 years of the greatest art form in the history of the world!

IV.   MUSINGS AND MUTTERINGS

Hmmmm....

For a multitude of reasons, the days of a multiplicity of options are nearing an end.

The Journey

This is what I've always believed...
This is what I've always wanted...
This is what I've always done...
This is who I've always been...

Up Until Now.

Change

"Doing it my way" is not always

    The best way,

It is often just habit, myopia

    Or stubbornness

Or, all of the above.

    Stay open.

Up Until Now

    I say, "But that's just

    How I am."

    My wiser self replies,

    "Up Until Now."

Good and Bad

Do "Do" what's Good for You

   And Don't "Do" what's Bad for you.

I Am

I Am Who I Am

I Do What I Do

When I can't Do It Anymore

I Stop Doing It ...

I've Already Done It.
I Have Nothing To Prove.

I am what I am
I do what I do

Don't tell me how I gotta be.

Got My ...

Got my wife
Got my house
Got my car
Got my friends
Got my pension
Got most of my health
I'm a very Lucky Man

Making It Better

Somehow There is Always a Way

To Make It Better.

Have the Courage

To Find It ...

And Do It.

Don't Sweat It ... Daily Life

Up the Steps
Down the Steps
Up the Steps
Down the Steps
Up the Steps Down the Steps

Just Do the Day

The Key

When all is said and done,
The ability to genuinely Give and Receive Love
Transcends Art, Adventure, and Freedom

Options

Keeping one's options open
Is not without cost.
It "costs" depth of commitment
To all that currently is
Or might be.

The Trick

The "secret to life" is successfully blending what
actually is with what you'd like it to be.

The trick is in fully and honestly assessing the
multiple truths of those seeming polarities.

In the Moment

We can't wait for everything to be better before beginning to live in the moment, and to live Life with Joy to the fullest. Whatever seems less than perfect, is still a part of living fully in the moment.
Now is Now is Now.

Wisdom

One mark of a truly independent person
Is knowing when they could actually use
Some help
And seeking it.

V.   GETTING CROTCHETY ... AND WISE?

Nope

I don't wanna.

I don't gotta.

They can't make me.

Overwhelmed

It's all too much …
Too many books to read
Too many movies to see
Too many songs to hear
Too many walks to take
Even too many friends to visit
Not enough time.

Being rendered inert
I sit in my chair with a smile.

I Was …

I was what I was

when I was …

now I ain't

Memorabilia

Sorting the Rummage
  Of My House and My Mind …

All Ya Got Is What'cha Got — I

As you near the end ...

All you got is what'cha got.

Ya got someone to love ya, or you don't.

Ya got a decent place to lay your head, or ya don't.

Ya got somethin' ya still like to do, or ya don't.

Ya got enough money to live OK, or ya don't.

Bein' old comes on ya damned sudden.

If ya had big dreams, ya should'a got'em by now.

It don't matter much anymore, who ya were or
what'cha done.

But keep smilin' … it's been a great ride.

Even If It Would Be Good For Me

At the ripe old age of 74, delayed gratification and long term goals

Are no longer my highest priorities

Christmas Changes

Grandkids growing up
Jihads going down
Brotherhood of man going…?
The Love and Joy
Of the Christmas season…

Mostly gone

All Ya Got Is What'cha Got — II

As you near the end....

All ya got is whatcha got...

Maybe it ain't the best ya ever had

Maybe ya blew it once or several times before

Maybe it ain't your dream vision

But now is now is now.

There probably ain't so much time.

How ya gonna spend it?

Regrettin' what ya don't have?

Regrettin' what ya might have lost

Regrettin' what ya might have blown?

Wishin' for or still Shootin' for the moon?

Or, being' just fine with whatcha got?

Living it fully.....

And all things bein' equal, Giving a nod of thanks to the Cosmos...

For whatcha got.

Taking it Easy

Nothing is a waste of my Time
When I now have Nothing to Do

Except what I want to Do

Which is just how I Like it to Be.

Waiting

At points in Time
When it may seem
Like nothing much matters
Except family, friends and health,
What Do we Daily Choose to Do
While Waiting for the End ...
Or for more Adventures to come?

Surprised Satisfaction

I'm happier now than I have ever been
Because I now have everything I never wanted.

Adventures

Two Kinds of Adventures …
Living them when we are young …
Writing about them when we are old.

Getting Older

The Ups and Downs
Yins and Yangs

Keeping the Up Times
In Your Mind and Heart.

The Golden Flowers …
The Sunrises ... the Sunsets …
The Smiles of Friends
The Love of Loved Ones
All the Adventures Yet to Come ...
Living to the Fullest …

Forever Young.

About the Author

BILL GRIVNA has been a teacher and professional actor/director for over 40 years. He is now Professor Emeritus in the Department of Theatre/Dance at Southern Illinois University Edwardsville. Bill is a former member of The Guthrie Theatre Company in Minneapolis. On film and television he has appeared as Dulinsky, a Polish immigrant, in director Ang Lee's feature film, *Ride with the Devil—the Director's Cut*, and in the TV mini-series, *Murder Ordained*, as Chappy. When he is not teaching theatre or acting and directing, Bill practices and teaches T'ai Chi, and is also a Life Skills Coach. As a writer, Bill's works include "The Journey," a chapter in a published anthology of memoirs titled *After the Academy*, a fairy tale or two, some beginning forays into short fiction, as well as a good many research proposals and reports.

63319674R00110

Made in the USA
Lexington, KY
04 May 2017